DYNAMIC PRACTICE DEVELOPMENT

Selling skills and techniques for the professions

KIM TASSO

THOROGOOD

Published by Thorogood
10-12 Rivington Street
London EC2A 3DU

Telephone: 020 7749 4748
Fax: 020 7729 6110
Email: info@thorogood.ws
Web: www.thorogood.ws

© Kim Tasso 2003

A CIP catalogue record for this book is
available from the British Library.

ISBN 1 85418 232 3

Cover and book designed by Driftdesign.

Printed in India by Replika Press Pvt. Ltd.

With love to James, Lizzie, Gilbert and Dad

About the author

KIM TASSO, BA (Hons) DipM MCIM MIDM MCIJ MBA, is an independent consultant, specialising in the professional services sector, with over 20 years' marketing experience. She attended her first sales training course in 1981 and although she only spent a limited – but successful – time in a field sales force in the computer industry she has been selling in one way or another ever since. She started her own consultancy in January 1994 and has worked for over 200 clients advising on and providing training and coaching in the strategic and operational aspects of marketing, selling and client development – including e-business strategies.

She was the first Director of Marketing at leading law firm Nabarro Nathanson between 1989 and 1993. Between 1987 and 1989, she was the first Marketing Manager at Deloitte Consulting (then called Touche Ross Management Consultants) and before this she was employed in the information technology sector by Honeywell Bull (now Groupe Bull), Logica and Comshare in a variety of sales and marketing roles.

She has an honours degree in psychology, a diploma in marketing, a diploma in professional coaching and mentoring and an MBA. She is a member of the Chartered Institute of Marketing (a Registered Marketer and a Registered Consultant), the Institute of Direct Marketing, the Chartered Institute of Journalists and the Institute of Directors.

Over 200 of her articles on marketing professional services have been published and she writes regularly for leading property and marketing magazines. She is a regular speaker and has lectured on postgraduate marketing courses. Other credits include writing the chapter on marketing for the Law Society's Probate Practitioners Handbook.

Illustrative clients

The Law Society, Olswang, Osborne Clarke, West London Training and Enterprise Council, Atis Real Weatheralls, Association of Personal Injury Lawyers, Psychology at Work, Tenon plc, Cole & Cole (now Morgan Cole), Manches, GVA Grimley, Wiggin & Co, 1 Brick Court, 4 Paper Buildings, Banner McBride (WPP Group plc), PriceWaterhouseCoopers, Lane & Partners, Mayer, Brown, Rowe & Maw.

Further information is available on her website at **www.kimtasso.com**

Contents

APPENDICES

List of figures

Preface

With thanks to all my former employers for the training and experience they gave me – in marketing, selling and life. Thanks to my clients, large and small, for having the confidence in my ability to help them and allowing me the opportunity to do so.

In particular I would like to thank the partners at Touche Ross Management Consultants (now Deloitte Consulting), Nabarro Nathanson, Olswang and Atis Real Weatheralls. Thanks also to all those people who have attended my presentations, training sessions and lectures and who gave me constructive feedback and the benefit of their experiences.

ONE
Introduction

ROADMAP

This chapter explains why the book was originally written in 1999 and how it has been updated. It offers a guide as to how it should be used by the professions whether inexperienced or expert at selling. It also describes the overall process of business development within a professional environment and describes the relationship between marketing, selling and client development. The chapter also addresses some key concepts, including whether selling is an art or a science and the central role of needs identification in successful selling. It concludes with an explanation of why you should have, or produce, a marketing plan before attempting to sell.

Objectives of the book

A visit to any local or virtual bookstore will reveal a treasury of books on selling and account management – so why another? Well, a number of reasons. The first is because my target audience – professional people in law, accountancy, surveying and consulting firms – rarely feel comfortable reading something that does not address their specific situation (e.g. professional rules, integrity, special client relationship, a dislike of the perceived 'hardness' of selling etc.) yet tend to prefer to build a base of knowledge from reading before venturing into other learning environments.

Second, rather than attempt to teach selling in a book my aim is to provide a review of as many different ideas and frameworks of selling as possible. Selling is such a vast subject – involving many different concepts and skills with so many competing approaches – that I have attempted – somewhat ambitiously – to provide a synthesis of the wide range of concepts and ideas that may be useful. Hopefully, this will save professionals much time (something they always value!) in identifying the ideas and frameworks most likely to be of value to them. The book also provides a resource for those in professional firms who are tasked with providing the necessary training, coaching and sales support in selling.

The third reason is that the professions are responsible for a huge chunk of the economy. There are over 70,000 solicitors, 200,000 accountants, 90,000 surveyors, 30,000 architects, 8,000 barristers, 5,000 actuaries and goodness knows how many consultants of one type or another in the UK alone. Yet there is little information about how they sell most effectively, the particular challenges they face and the approaches that offer the most value. Other high value service providers (e.g. PR agents, advertising executives etc.) share many of the same challenges.

Fourth, most of the professions deal in long-term client relationships. This means that there must be a natural linkage and balance between developing their reputation and understanding their markets (marketing), winning new business (selling) and developing business from existing clients (account management) which often comprises over 80% of a professional firms' annual income. Although many of the techniques and skills are the same, there are differences in how they are applied in new or existing client situations and many professionals feel much more comfortable with existing client relationships.

PSF-ing is selling: This is one of the tougher hurdles for conventional denizens of departments to surmount.
That is, realising that Sales is US. (It was damn difficult for official professional service firms, such as the Big Five accountancies to deal with this only a few years ago.
Now they've become first class prostitutes.)

TOM PETERS
THE PROFESSIONAL SERVICE FIRM 50

My final reason is that I firmly believe that selling is relatively easy to those people who have the integrity to act in a professional manner and who are genuinely interested in helping clients by providing solutions to problems they face – or walking away when they cannot. The professions seek only to serve their clients interests well whilst making a profit. As a marketer, my aim is to anticipate and meet client needs thus generating a profit. Marketers and the professions therefore seek the same thing. Professional selling means putting the clients and their needs above all else – although the long-term aim is profit from a satisfied client. I want to convince professionals that they do not need to do anything distasteful or dishonourable in order to win business. Integrity is as important in selling as in any other aspect of professional life.

I have found that it is often only a professional's misconceptions and lack of confidence in selling that holds them back. Selling – once you have found a style and the tools that suit your personality – can be as interesting, satisfying and as important as any other aspect of your professional life. I hope to convince you.

The first edition of this book (which was published as an Executive Report and is still available) contained information from a research study I conducted into the attitudes towards selling amongst senior professionals. Yet these attitudes have changed so significantly over the past three years – there is a much wider acceptance now of the need for effective selling within the professions. Selling is no longer a dirty word and it has crept onto the internal training schedules in recent years. Therefore, in response to feedback from readers of the Report I have replaced the research section with a short overview of marketing techniques and some practical guidance on producing a marketing plan as this is a significant factor in increasing later sales effectiveness. The original version contained around 40,000 words and this edition has a massive 67,000 words – so a major overhaul and update has been undertaken and some of the newest and latest thinking and ideas – from the academics as well as the leading practitioners – have now been incorporated.

How to use this book

A beginner

You could read this book from start to finish – in doing so you will obtain a comprehensive introduction and overview of a huge amount of material about marketing and selling professional services to new and existing clients. This is a recommended route for those readers who have had little prior experience or training in selling techniques. It is also the recommended route for those who feel uncomfortable with the idea of selling a professional service. The book is like a menu, identify those areas that feel comfortable to you and adopt them – leave alone those elements that you dislike. There is no one right way to sell, different approaches and techniques suit different people and different situations.

An expert

More experienced readers will find the book valuable as a reference work. You may want to do a fast track read by skipping the first three introductory sections and starting at Chapter four (The buyers' point of view). Alternatively, you can quickly read the 'Roadmap' at the start of each chapter to see the main themes that are covered and to whom and when they might be most useful.

Specific question

You may have a specific question or issue in selling you wish to address in which case you should consult the table below. Or you may wish to refer to the book when a particular situation emerges in the future – most likely when you are pitching for new business or trying to develop more work from an existing client and there are specific chapters on these topics (see Chapters seven and eight).

YOUR SPECIFIC QUESTION OR ISSUE	SECTIONS OF THE BOOK THAT WILL BE OF MOST VALUE
Do all professionals feel as negatively about selling as I do?	Chapters one and three.
How do I develop more confidence in selling?	There are two routes to confidence – the first is to invest time in learning more about selling – you need to read this entire book carefully. The second thing is practice, which is in your hands.
Why is selling in the professions different?	See Chapter three.
What is the difference between marketing and selling?	This is addressed both in Chapter one (Introduction) and three (What is selling?).
I have been advising one client for a very long time but why do I never get any additional work from them?	Chapter eight on account management provides a structured approach to developing more work from an existing client.
How can I win this pitch?	This topic is dealt with extensively in Chapter seven on competitive tendering.

YOUR SPECIFIC QUESTION OR ISSUE	SECTIONS OF THE REPORT THAT WILL BE OF MOST VALUE
But isn't it better to concentrate on your existing clients rather than chasing new business?	You need to do both – read about the context of relationship management in Chapter one (Introduction). Developing existing clients is covered extensively in Chapter eight (Account management).
But aren't good salespeople born rather than made?	An interesting argument. Read about the attributes of a good salesperson (see Chapter three – What is selling?).

Management or functional responsibility

As a senior partner with responsibility for selling in your firm, you will find that Chapter nine (Firm wide issues on selling) offers an overview of the firm wide actions that must be taken to facilitate selling success by the individuals in your firm. If you have been tasked with establishing sales training programmes within your organisation, you will find Chapter five (Selling frameworks) and six (Selling skills) of most value to assist you in your quest.

Why do professionals dislike selling?

Reasons why selling is different for the professions is explored at length in Chapter three (What is selling?).

However, one of the main reasons we dislike selling is because our perception of selling is tainted by the poor experiences of selling we have experienced as consumers at the hands of poorly trained, unethical and pushy 'salespeople'. When selling is effective we are hardly aware that it is happening because it feels natural, we have a rapport with and trust the person helping us to buy and we end up pleased with what we have purchased. Good selling means you must have empathy with your prospect and you must be careful to match what you promote with what they need:

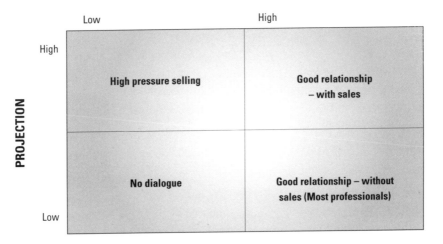

FIGURE 1: WHY PROFESSIONALS DON'T LIKE SELLING

How you develop empathy and 'project' effectively and appropriately is at the heart of all good selling and these topics are dealt with extensively in this book.

Another key issue is the professionals' in-built fear of failure. A professional is someone who is revered by clients and who is perceived as an expert –

they cannot be seen to fail! Professionals are risk averse and selling can be a risky business. Fear of failure is also a very British thing. In the United States, you are not considered a viable business person until you have at least one decent business failure under your belt.

The professions are wary of making mistakes. The premiums we must pay for professional indemnity insurance are a reminder of the cost associated with mistakes – in cash, time and reputation terms. In marketing and selling there are no hard and fast rules. As most professions have to learn about marketing and selling they are likely to make mistakes – you rarely learn anything without making some errors. Yet the professions are rather unforgiving, in most firms they have short memories for great successes and long memories of even minor errors. No wonder the prospect of selling strikes such fear into the hearts of even seasoned professionals.

There is also a fear of embarrassment. To be seen to be marketing and selling is uncomfortable for some. You are stepping out of your usual role and you are not quite sure what is expected and what is acceptable. In the past, if you were a good lawyer or accountant the phone would always ring with new clients and new work. In those days, when professional rules forbade promotion, it was almost an admission of failure to be seen to be 'touting' for business. The market has changed now – it is really competitive – even the best professionals must dedicate time and energy to marketing to maintain a flow of work.

Although there is a risk of failure in selling, the risks can be minimised with training, planning and practice. At the end of the day, selling is a bit like playing a computer game – if you lose you can always start a new game. As a very senior partner at a leading firm of consultants said jokingly to me recently: "Selling is like playing Tomb Raider – if Lara gets killed it is not the end of the world. You just start that bit of the game again and progress to the next stage with the added experience of what to avoid in the future!". In effect, by making small mistakes you can avoid making the really big ones! Selling is like life, and, as they say, life is a journey.

The context of client relationship management (CRM)

This book is focused on selling skills, yet it is written by a marketing professional (admittedly one who started her career in selling). Although the book focuses on selling it is very much in the context of an overall model of client relationship management (CRM). The figure below shows that marketing, selling and client or account management are part of the same ongoing and integrated process within a professional firm.

Marketing
- 'Broadcast'
- General needs
- Research
- Brand and profile building
- One to many

Selling
- Converting enquiries
- Responding to pitches/tenders
- Specific needs
- One to one

Client development
- Retaining and developing existing client
- Cross selling
- Account management
- Many to one

FIGURE 2: THE BUSINESS DEVELOPMENT PROCESS IN A PROFESSIONAL FIRM
(© KIM TASSO 2000)

It is not that different from the old professional model of 'finders, minders and grinders'. It can also be viewed as the processes mapped alongside the usual model of relationship management:

FIGURE 3: BUILDING CLIENT RELATIONSHIPS

Yet selling to a new client or to a private client as opposed to a commercial client is different to the way we sell to a long established existing client. The way we approach an informal first meeting is different to the way we approach a formal competitive tendering process. So we must consider the various skills and models in terms of the very different situations in which professionals must sell. This is part of the rationale for this book.

The art and science of selling

Is selling an art or a science? It is both. Obviously, some people are born with personalities and attributes that make it easier for them to communicate with others and to build rapport and trust quickly. Therefore, they find it relatively easy to sell. Others have to work hard at selling as these things do not come so naturally.

There is no magic formula that you can apply to any marketing or selling situation that will guarantee success. But there are tried and tested frameworks, tools and concepts that provide considerable help in achieving success. Yet these frameworks and tools must be used judiciously, with due regard to the people, the organisations and the specific situations in which they are used. The science blended with the art.

Cultural differences

There are big cultural differences in the areas of marketing and selling. For example, most US law firms comprise a series of partners who are extremely effective at selling – but relatively poor at the combined effort of marketing their firms and practice areas. Similarly, the very up front and direct approach to requesting business in the United States feels too direct to be comfortable to those in the UK. When you look across Europe you find that there are further complexities and if you hope to sell to Middle Eastern or Japanese clients then you are looking at a whole different ballgame. So please take care when your selling requires you to deal with such diversity.

Similarly, agents within property firms are much better at selling in particular transactions than their colleagues in the valuation, building surveying or rating teams. In law and accountancy, there are differences in the style adopted when selling transactional services (e.g. mergers and acquisitions, project finance, litigation etc.) than in ongoing services (e.g. audit, commercial). There are differences between those professions who have to sell in the public sector as opposed to the private sector.

Understanding the buyers' attitudes and the buying process will enable you to adapt your style and approach to suit. There is no 'one size fits all' in selling – you need to be inside the mind of the buyer. This is the reason that developing empathy is so important in effective selling. This can be particularly hard when the buyer is from a different cultural, organisational or educational background.

The importance of needs

 Without a need there can be no sale.

I have said this at every training course I have ever given. This is where I believe the professions have most to learn. The essence of selling is to get into the mind of the person you are talking to and to find out what they need – both in their business roles and as individual human beings.

Clients need solutions to business problems but they are also people who need to interact with their professional advisers in a particular way. You might have the best business or financial solution but if you do not meet their personal needs in terms of how you communicate and deliver that solution, you will fail to sell. You might get on with the person very well, but fail to see how your expertise in litigation or surveying will provide a solution to a business need that they have.

Trying to sell when there is no need is unprofessional. This book will not provide assistance for such situations and I strongly urge you to consider your professional ethics if you attempt to do so. However, there are techniques that will help you with background research and communication that may help you – through structured discussions with your clients – discover and develop a need that you can then attempt to meet.

Increasingly in the professions, the selling task must first focus on educating clients on what their needs might or should be – the professional, much like a consultant, must therefore help the client identify a problem and shape and define it. This requires good skills in research, questioning, listening and problem definition – all of which are covered in this book.

Marketing is the management process for anticipating and fulfilling client needs profitably. Selling is the part of the marketing process that consummates this process.

Why you should have a coherent marketing strategy

This book is concerned with selling. Yet selling rarely takes place in a vacuum. Selling is made much easier and is more successful if it is undertaken within the context of a coherent strategic marketing plan. Most people in the professions cannot see any difference between marketing and selling. To be fair, the distinction is a fine one. In essence, marketing is the process of analysis and research you apply to whole groups of people with a common need (a market). Selling is where there is a specific need with one organisation or individual. Marketing also contains the all important marketing communication programmes – or promotional activity – that builds brands, raises awareness, educates, initiates the dialogue and creates opportunities to meet which then become a selling opportunity.

For many years, the professions have done their selling as individuals within a practice which is home to several partners who all build their own client bases individually and separately. Of course this model still works today. However, the increasing sophistication of those firms who have well researched and carefully constructed strategic marketing plans, which ensure groups of partners work together in the same direction, enjoy greater selling success and greater profitability. If you do not have a marketing plan it would be a good idea to prepare one before you embark on a selling programme – it will save you much time, money and heartache.

Chapter two provides a short introduction to marketing which you should use before you start selling if there is no existing marketing plan.

TWO
Marketing planning

ROADMAP

This chapter provides a fast, brief introduction to the fundamental concepts of marketing. It provides an overview of the various marketing tools such as advertising, public relations, direct marketing and sales promotion. It also provides a step-by-step framework to help you build a marketing plan if you do not possess one.

Understanding the basic principles of marketing

Introduction

One of the keys to successful marketing is having a sound marketing plan at the outset. The marketing plan entails a careful analysis of your current internal strengths and the external market (the prospects, the competition and the demand) so that you can develop the right awareness in that market so that your subsequent sales efforts are received favourably.

What is marketing?

Marketing is the management process responsible for anticipating and meeting client needs profitably.

This is the official definition of marketing from the Chartered Institute of Marketing (CIM) and one that few professionals would argue with – after all, isn't every lawyer or accountant there to meet the needs of their clients whilst making a modest profit? But the definition is of little value on its own.

Marketing operates at three levels. First, there is a marketing function. Someone within your practice needs to take overall responsibility for marketing to ensure that the appropriate resources are available, that all the different marketing activities throughout the firm happen in a co-ordinated and effective way and to manage the various marketing information systems that you need to draw upon. It is also helpful to have a source of marketing expertise on which all members of the firm can draw to ensure that marketing mistakes do not occur. This source of expertise may be provided by external consultants or agencies.

Second, marketing is a philosophy that focuses – at every point in the firm – on the needs of the client. This is apparent when we consider the importance of internal marketing. From a cross-selling perspective we must ensure everyone knows what each professional team has to offer, its particular strengths and weaknesses and how to introduce clients to the services available. From a service delivery perspective, every member of the firm who has contact with the client (whether as a receptionist, switchboard operator, secretary, trainee etc.) creates an impression about the firm and either supports or undermines the firm's overall brand or service promise.

Third, marketing is a series of tools and techniques (for example, advertising, direct mail, publications, selling, etc.) designed to do different marketing tasks and these are described further below.

Marketing typically comprises a number of elements that are blended together into what is called 'the marketing mix'. The elements are:

- **Product**: the legal, accountancy or property expertise and the way in which that advice is processed and delivered. It is important to recognise that lay clients are often unable to determine whether the advice is good or poor and will therefore assess the quality of advice on the basis of the way in which that advice is delivered.

- **Place**: the market where the services are promoted and delivered or the channels involved e.g. web based services.

- **Price**: very often professionals price their services on the basis of what it costs to produce and deliver, yet issues such as perceived value and competition will have a major impact.

- **Promotion**: all those marketing communication activities designed to alert clients and potential clients to the services and benefits available.

- **Physical evidence**: the way your offices, promotional material and staff appear.

- **Process**: the way in which you produce and deliver the work – quality systems and procedures are critical here.

- **People**: the fee-earners and their support staff who are the marketers, sellers, producers and deliverers of the services.

These different elements are explored further in the remainder of this chapter but it is important that all elements are considered together – a promotional campaign alone is unlikely to succeed.

There is often some confusion within the professions about the terms 'marketing', 'selling' and 'business development'. They are distinct activities aimed at different parts of an ongoing and integrated cycle – see figure 2 on page 9 in Chapter one.

So what is selling?

Marketing is concerned with identifying needs in the market (therefore research and analysis are important), identifying or developing the services that meet those needs (e.g. service or market development) and communicating the appropriate messages to the market. It is where the firm 'broadcasts' a message to many members of a market (for example, a market might be all the wealthy people within a 10-mile radius or it might be all the banks with international clients). Marketing would also be concerned with developing the reputation or brand of the organisation, service or individual. Typically, marketing is conducted by those who have some training in marketing – for example, professional marketing staff, designers, copywriters, PR experts and so on. If marketing is successful, enquiries will be generated.

When you move from communicating with a market to communicating with a particular organisation or individual you have moved into the selling phase. Here the focus is on the specific needs of that one organisation or individual rather than the generalised needs of the whole market. Some argue that selling is more orientated to 'pushing' the product or service you want to sell although most successful selling is driven by the needs of the buyer. Typically in a professional firm, selling is the preserve of the most senior fee-earners – they have the experience and knowledge to promote their own and the firm's benefits. Sometimes, there is a formal tendering process (or beauty parade) involved if there is a large volume of work or a panel of approved providers at the client organisation.

Converting a prospect through successful selling results in a client. However, one set of instructions does not a client make. The continued marketing and selling to that client (within the framework of CRM – Client Relationship Management) ensures further instructions are received for additional or new services. This is a vital activity in every professional firm as usually around 80 per cent of a firm's annual income is from existing clients. Typically, this area of client or account development is where the majority of professionals focus their efforts. In the past it was common to say:

> *The only marketing we need do is a really good job for our existing clients.*

This view of marketing should dispel the myth that it is only about new business – a major component of professional firm marketing is about developing existing clients and the referrer base through relationship marketing.

B2C/business-to-consumer verses B2B/business-to-business marketing

In the professions, we usually refer to B2C marketing as 'private client' marketing and B2B as 'commercial client' marketing. The difference is important.

The marketing techniques you should use vary depending on the nature of your target client. We must also consider the importance of segmenting the market into smaller, more manageable segments with common characteristics or needs. Clever segmentation can result in a highly profitable niche practice – which makes achieving a premium fee for specialist work much easier.

Some professionals (e.g. personal injury lawyers, wills and probate lawyers, accountants offering help with tax returns etc.) are promoting their services to private individuals or families. There are over 58 million people in the UK and they can be grouped by socio-economic group, by age, by location, by household, by lifestyle and in various other ways. Even though you have focused on a particular group, it would be difficult and not very cost effective to try to mail all members of that group or to spend hours in one-to-one meetings with them. So, more indirect methods of marketing might usefully be adopted – such as advertising or media relations.

The members of each group or segment will have common interests or needs that you can address within a marketing campaign. The smaller and more focused your segment the easier it will be to reach the members with a suitable marketing tool and the easier it will be to tailor your message to address their specific needs.

Some elements of the private client market are keen to use the Internet – and there are a number of examples of successful websites that provide an efficient on-line solution to some professional services. Similarly, other elements of the private client market might appreciate a much greater level of face-to-face interaction when dealing with professional matters – perhaps even in their own home environment. By segmenting the market we can tailor the service, the price and the promotional activity more precisely to their needs.

The majority of professionals will, however, be targeting commercial or other organisations. There are significantly fewer businesses than individuals in the country and there is a great wealth of information about them in various public directories and publications, and on-line. Business people are less likely to be reached effectively through advertising so you might adopt a more direct approach to marketing to this group – by direct mail, through seminars or perhaps by having a professional visit them. Their needs will be different too – private individuals require different things from their professional advisers than businesses. Often private individuals will be relatively inexperienced at purchasing professional services, whereas their commercial counterparts are more likely to be experts in the services they are buying. So, the way of reaching the business audience needs to be different and the message you communicate needs to be different.

A further alternative might be that you decide to target referrer organisations to generate new business. This is particularly the case where your professional service is of a one-off or transactional nature. So corporate finance professionals or architects may find their marketing programmes targeting referrer or intermediary organisations. Here the business-to-business techniques are more likely to be effective.

As a rule of thumb (there are always exceptions!), if you are marketing to consumers you use indirect methods and for organisations you use more direct approaches. The following table shows the various techniques that would perform these tasks:

INDIRECT METHODS	DIRECT METHODS
Advertising	Networking
Signs/posters	Selling (presentations and visits)
Media relations	Tenders
Sponsorship	Direct marketing
Literature (left on display)	Literature (mailed)
Websites	Seminars/briefings
Word of mouth	Hospitality
	Telemarketing
	E-marketing

Different levels of marketing planning

It is important to realise that marketing plans are needed for different levels of a professional firm:

- The global business/marketing plan (e.g. brand).

- The UK (or other European country) business/marketing plan.

- The plan for a particular office or location.

- The plan for a particular market sector (e.g. all technology companies or all agricultural organisations).

- The plan for a particular professional department (e.g. corporate finance, tax etc).

- For a particular partner or fee-earner.

Therefore, decide for which level you are producing a plan and obtain plans for other levels in your firm first to provide you with guidance, but also to ensure that your plan integrates and reinforces with others' plans.

A marketing framework

Having reviewed the main marketing ideas, what follows now is a framework to guide you through the various steps you should take to prepare yourself and your firm for effective marketing and to prepare a marketing plan to focus on your marketing, selling and client development activities. It may seem that a lot of analysis, thinking and planning has to take place before you get to any real 'action'. However, most professional firms' marketing fails because insufficient attention is paid to precisely these issues.

Analysing your present situation
(A marketing audit or situational analysis)

Analysing your current work, clients and sources

You should start by analysing what clients you serve at present and how those clients came to your firm. Were they generated by external marketing activities, referrals from other organisations or individuals or by referrals from people within your firm? The more detail you obtain on the type of clients you currently serve, why and how they came to your firm and what they value about your service the easier it will be to identify the appropriate marketing methods to adopt in the future.

You could prepare a diagram to provide a map of where the work comes from. If your firm does not have this information then an early priority is to ensure that systems (usually a client and contact database and a work referral or lead tracking system) are established to collect this information in the future (see Chapter nine on Firm-wide issues). Marketing without sound information is rather like building on sand – it is without foundation and liable to crumble away. But don't get too hung up on the accuracy of information available – general trends will do.

Understanding your major sources of work will help you develop a strategy to focus your marketing efforts in those areas where they are most likely to bear fruit. You cannot possibly market to all sources and markets effectively so you will need to make choices. Your choices should be based on information as accurate and as up-to-date as possible. You need to know the amount of fee income, the type of work, the profitability and the importance to the firm (e.g. to other departments) of each type of work.

Sometimes the information might provide ideas about potential markets you should explore. Sometimes the market changes and the past client information does not provide clues for future action. There are other marketing approaches that will help in these circumstances.

The analysis should provide you with three or four areas on which you need to concentrate. Or it may show you that your marketing challenge is to radically alter the nature of clients and work you are generating. Once you have identified the types of clients, or referrers, you want to target, you should start collecting information about them. This should include their names and addresses, their needs and concerns, any links within your firm, background information about them and ideas on how you might approach them, or build the relationship if they are existing clients.

If you have the time available, you will find talking to a number of existing clients and referrers an invaluable aid to future marketing. Client research will help you to identify why people come to your firm, what they like (and don't like) about the service, what additional help or advice they would like and what it is about your firm that is different from others. Time and effort spent investigating the perceptions and satisfaction of existing clients is always paid back.

It is important to ensure that when talking to clients and referrers you do not concentrate alone on the services they currently use. You must adopt the client's point of view, as very often the reason they will value your firm will be more than your expertise in one particular specialism.

Reviewing your skills, staff and services

Your people are your product or your service. They are producers of the professional work and the mechanism by which that professional work is delivered to clients (unless you are making extensive use of the Internet for service delivery).

So the next thing is to review the skills and abilities of the staff that are promoting, doing and delivering the professional advice. Do they have any specialist expertise? If your firm has some expertise that is unlikely to be found in comparable firms then you are on your way to finding a key point of difference (USP or Unique Selling Proposition) which will make targeting and marketing much easier.

Are there any gaps in your expertise? It is important to be clear if there are any areas where your advice is likely to be less than optimal – either training or skills development is required (i.e. product development) or you need to steer your marketing away from these areas and onto other stronger offerings.

Are your staff able and motivated to sell? (See Chapters four and nine for more information on motivation.) Perhaps you need to consider some interpersonal skills training to develop their enthusiasm and confidence for generating new business? Perhaps you need to review the rewards system so that they are encouraged to invest time and energy in winning new business? Even if you decide to take on the major share of marketing yourself, you will still need to ensure that all those who have contact with clients understand what you are trying to achieve, deliver the services in the way you have promised and achieve a high level of client satisfaction.

Looking at the market

Now you understand where your work comes from, and the resources you have to develop and deliver work in the future, you must look outside your firm to the local market.

You start by assessing local demands and needs. The demand in your area may be different to that in other parts of the country depending on, for example in private client marketing, the demographic socio-economic spread of the local population and the prevailing attitudes towards planning and professional advice of the local people. You can obtain this information either by research at local reference libraries or by seeking help from your local Training and Enterprise Council (TEC or Business Link) who often have concise overviews of areas and information on the main economic and social trends. Networking at local events will also enable you to learn about the dynamics within your marketplace and will provide vital marketing intelligence. It will have the added benefit of raising your firm's profile for all its services.

In commercial markets you will need to develop your understanding of key business issues – perhaps even focusing on particular types or sizes of business or particular industry sectors. You will need to think much broader than you have done so previously – think beyond your type of professional advice and think about the current and emerging business, economic, political and technological issues. Again, the TECs may have useful information for you or you may find it useful to speak to local Chambers of Commerce or business, trade and commercial associations in your area.

It is important to remember that effective marketing requires you to identify and anticipate needs. Without a need it will be impossible to sell anything. Be objective when researching and considering needs within a market. You may have to rethink the nature and packaging of the services you are providing – e.g. parcelling up a number of professional and other services to be different from what your firm has offered in the past. There have been some interesting examples where, for example, lawyers providing personal injury advice have linked with insurance and financial service providers and even those involved in rehabilitation and planning specialists where accommodation changes are likely to be needed. You must think from the buyer's point of view who will not necessarily be aware of, or interested in, professional divides. Clients have needs that span professional, financial and other types of advice.

A key issue to consider will obviously be the strengths and weaknesses, strategies and activities of your competitors. These may not all be professionals. In any market you will face a variety of competitors. And there may be competition from unusual sources – such as on-line help through the Internet, non-professional advisers (e.g. licensed conveyancers for legal property advice, insurance companies for legal cover, mortgage lenders for property advice etc). The key will be to identify the main ones and develop your strategies accordingly. Information about your competitors is not sufficient. You must use this information to modify your approach and activities in order to find a different marketing position offering different benefits.

Pulling your research together

An analysis of your internal strengths and weaknesses and how these translate into external opportunities and threats will help identify the key issues on which you need to act.

As you consider each opportunity and threat think what you need to do – as a specific action – to resolve or grasp the situation. The more time you spend on synthesising the key findings of your internal and external research, the easier it will be to develop a marketing strategy and action plan that works for you.

At this point you may have many different options and ideas to pursue. But a key element of a successful marketing strategy is to select and focus on just one or two of these – you simply will not have the time and resources to tackle all the ideas you identify.

Deciding what works for you

Setting objectives

First you must determine what your firm's overall objectives are – both in terms of financial targets (what fee income and profit contribution is expected?) and in terms of the reputation, perception and impression the firm wishes to create in the market, and the nature of the key clients it wishes to target. It is at this stage that some professionals may find a difficulty – especially if the firm is focusing on developing both commercial clients and private clients. It may also be difficult if there are other practice groups targeting similar client and referrer groups to those targeted by your team. You will need to work together carefully in this case to produce an integrated plan for marketing.

Once you have identified the firm-wide objectives and the short-term (usually one year forward and based on utilisation, fee income and profit) objectives, you can start to draft some more specific long- and short-term objectives for your team. Setting objectives that are measurable and realistic (see Chapter six) is hard but without them it will be difficult to focus your marketing efforts appropriately and impossible to measure the success.

Selecting your targets

With clear objectives set, it will help considerably if you can be as specific as possible about the amount and type of work you hope to obtain from existing clients and contacts (in the short term) and from new clients in the longer-term.

Producing lists of referrer organisations, the names of existing clients and other detailed information at this stage will save much time later. Again, such lists will focus the mind and help you assess whether your marketing is working effectively. You can produce these lists as a department or office but it will also be useful to ask each fee-earner to produce their own lists.

Agreeing a strategy

Marketing strategy is a huge subject in its own right but this is a book about selling so we can only touch on the subject. In essence, your marketing strategy is about which products or service you plan to promote into which markets. It involves choices. Once you have selected your services (which, if new, requires a product or service development strategy) and your markets (which, if new, require a market development strategy) you need to agree the basis of your competitive thrust (cost leadership or differentiation) and market positioning.

Position in the market

From previous studies into professional services marketing, a common mistake is to try to be all things to all people. For example, lawyers often try to provide a high quality, high added-value service at the lowest possible price. Not only is this a recipe for working 24 hours a day with no return but also for financial disaster!

Leading business advisers suggest that there are a limited number of choices – either to aim for a broad or narrow (niche) market and to compete either on the basis of cost leadership, or on the basis of some differentiation (but not both together!).

You need to decide what position you want to achieve in the market. If all the other providers are pushing the low cost, pre-packaged 'product' then look at whether there are opportunities for firms offering a higher priced, more tailored 'service'. If others are targeting the low-income families, consider targeting the wealthy. If others are focusing on reaching the 'man in the street', why not consider reaching the executive in the boardroom or local employers? The same with commercial clients – what specific group or segment of the market can you target – those within a particular market sector? With a particular type of legal structure or funding? With a particular type of business problem? (E.g. overseas exporters, employers of a larger number of contractor staff etc).

A key element of your positioning will be trying to identify what it is that you offer that others don't – it may be expertise in a particular area, it may be your accessibility, it may be your client care philosophy, it may be your level of computerisation (e.g. web delivery) or the degree of integration with other professional and financial services. Unless you are pursuing a 'cost leadership' strategy, you will need to identify a suitable differentiation strategy. Many firms will try to develop a 'brand' to help communicate some real or perceived difference in their service – perhaps based around their particular style of client relationships.

The following diagrams may assist you in developing your positioning ideas:

Hugh Davidson
(Eight most significant potential competitive advantages)

- Superior product/service benefits
- Perceived advantage
- Low cost operations

- Superior knowledge (e.g. better research or information systems)
- Scale advantages
- Offensive attitudes

MAYSON'S SOURCES OF VALUE

What will clients pay you for – rather than paying someone else?

- Personal relationship
- Local knowledge or proximity
- High level of specialisation (technical expertise or market)
- Your ability to co-ordinate services

- Absolute mass (being the biggest)
- Processing (for volume matters)
- Information engineering (packaging and publishing the knowledge)

You might decide to base your positioning on the basis of a single major benefit such as: best quality, best performance, most reliable, most durable, safest, fastest, best value for money, least expensive, most prestigious, best designed or styles, easiest to use or most convenient.

If you intend to achieve competitive differentiation and market positioning through branding you must develop your knowledge of branding, as it is a vast subject in its own right and often confused with visual and corporate identity.

> *A successful brand is an identifiable product, service, person or place augmented in such a way that the buyer or user perceives relevant, unique added values which match their needs most closely. Furthermore, its success results from being able to sustain these added values in the face of competition.*
>
> **LESLIE DE CHERNATORY AND MALCOLM MCDONALD**

It is important that your strategy takes a slightly longer-term view as well. You already have financial targets for the next year so use the positioning stage to identify where you want your practice area to be in say, three of four years' time. It will take this long for the market to learn and understand a new positioning statement.

Place (and segmentation)

There are two market 'place' issues for you to consider as part of your strategy. The first issue is which markets you are targeting. You may adopt a penetration strategy to gain more work in an existing market or you may decide to try and enter new markets.

Having completed your analysis of existing clients, sources and work you will have hopefully identified some specific markets or sectors on which you will focus. This process of breaking a market into smaller segments is called segmentation. It is important for smaller firms who do not have the resources of their larger competitors and because it makes it easier to tailor your expertise, benefits and messages to the needs of that specific segment or niche. We talked above about two key sectors for the professions – commercial and private clients, but there are many approaches to segmenting a market – geographical, market sector, size, value and so on. Bonoma and Shapiro identified the following ways to segment industrial or commercial markets:

- Demographic: industry, company, location.
- Operating variables: technology, user status, client capabilities.
- Purchasing approaches: buying criteria, buying policies, current relationships.
- Situational factors: urgency, size of contract, applications.
- Personal characteristics: loyalty, attitudes to risk.

The other aspect of 'place' is the channels you use to reach the market. Some firms, for example, have invested heavily in technology so that the Internet (through portals, websites or extranets) are the main mechanism by which their professional services are delivered.

Packaging the product and the people

An integral part of deciding your strategy and positioning will be agreeing what it is you are selling in the market. Some firms have differentiated their services by packaging together a range of services or products – some from within their firms and some from alliance partners or other third parties.

The actual core 'product' is similar in all such packages – what differs is the particular needs of the particular target audience being addressed and the emphasis. Another approach might be to package the way you offer or deliver the advice – for example, there are some highly innovative websites which offer a fixed price procedure for straightforward professional services.

In addition to packaging what you are actually offering, you need to consider the way in which you deliver the advice and this involves taking a long and hard look at everyone (fee-earners, technical support assistants, secretaries and switchboard staff etc.) involved in client communications. Lay clients are unlikely to be able to tell whether they are getting good or bad advice from their professional advisers (they will take it for granted that you can practice in the area in which you are qualified), so they will infer your 'quality' through the impressions that are generated by the way in which you answer the 'phone, the speed with which their queries are answered, the accuracy and layout of the letters and documents they receive, the friendliness of the professional and support staff they meet and the tidiness and comfort of the reception areas and office they visit.

Increasingly, within the professions, there are thoughts that knowledge and information will be the key to competitive positioning and the nature of professional services/products, as well as a key indicator of strong and successful client relationships (see Chapter eight on Account management):

Developing knowledge based client relationships
The future of professional services (Ross Dawson)

- 'Greatest value to clients has been in making them more knowledgeable'
  - Better decisions enhance business capabilities

- Death knell for 'black box'

- Various channels for knowledge transfer

- New models for pricing knowledge based services

- Information can be digitised, knowledge is intrinsic to people and thus the continuing importance of rich ongoing informal interactions in professional client relationships.

Getting everyone to be a valued and integral part of your service promise will require training, communication and involvement in the marketing, planning and implementation process so if you haven't involved them so far, do so now. This can be achieved through team meetings where you explain what you are trying to achieve and ask them to discuss the barriers they perceive and the help they require in delivering the promise. An alternative approach would be to appoint people to specialist roles – such as handling telephone enquiries, explaining the service or first meeting management.

Pricing

Clients will choose on price alone if they perceive no other differences in what is being offered by different suppliers. Therefore, if there is no perceived difference in the professional service offered by your firm or any other provider, then price will dominate the decision as it is perceived as a commodity. Remember the need to make a decision between trying to offer 'cost leadership' service in the market (i.e. the cheapest) and providing something different or better. The above section on strategy will assist.

A key element of marketing is to move clients away from thinking about the price to thinking about the benefits of the service and other factors – such as speed, accessibility, ease of use, friendliness, personal service, etc.

The price must equate to the value of the service as perceived by clients. They are not interested in the cost of providing that service (i.e. how much time you take to produce a perfect document). Therefore, you must think of price in both strategic terms (what are my broad hourly or fixed fee rates and what level of profitability do I wish to achieve?) and in tactical terms (how much for this particular piece of work?). Some firms are becoming more creative in pricing, moving away from hourly rates to fixed price deals, value billing, retainer arrangements, insurance deals, shared risk arrangements and bonus arrangements. These are often designed to give clients the benefits of certainty.

Promotion and internal marketing

At last we get to the phase with which most professional people will be more familiar – the promotion and selling of the services they provide. The objectives and earlier analysis should reveal where your efforts are to be focused and should have indicated the types of marketing tool that are going to be most effective in achieving them.

The following section identifies some of the key issues to consider when planning to use some of the most common marketing tools. You might seek further information and advice from marketing books (see Appendix two for a list of possible books to help).

Advertising

Advertising is where you pay a media owner (e.g. a directory, a newspaper, a magazine, a radio station, a poster site operator, a TV channel, a website portal) to reproduce your message exactly as you require. There are two elements to the cost – the cost of designing and producing the advert artwork and the cost of the medium's space.

Advertising is a tool to get a simple message to a large audience that is perhaps difficult to reach by other means. It is generally more suited to winning private client work. Common places where professional firms advertise for private client work include telephone directories, local newspapers and poster sites near advice centres.

There are over 1,400 trade and technical journals which are targeted at specific business, professional or trade audiences. For example, there are magazines aimed at funeral directors, nursing home staff, those who care for the elderly and accountants. There are over 60 different property magazines (both commercial and private), an equal number of financial magazines and many more computer magazines. You should look in the reference section of your library for directories such as Willis or BRAD to obtain more details of the vast array of specialist media.

One-off adverts are rarely effective so if advertising is your chosen tool then make sure adverts will appear on more than one occasion over a suitable period of time. You must be clear of the following before you attempt any advertising:

- Who is my target audience and what media might reach them efficiently?
- What message am I trying to convey?
  - Is it simple and clear?

- Does it focus on a specific need and mention benefits?
- Is it sufficiently different from other professionals' advertisements?

- Does my advert have impact?
- Does it convey the right image of my firm and the particular service promoted?
- What action does it prompt the reader/viewer to take?
- Is there a more cost effective way to reach my target audience?

With all marketing activities, you should be sure you can respond to any enquiries that are generated (have your switchboard and reception staff been briefed?) and that you can measure the response from any specific activity to assess its effectiveness.

Most professional firms focus on display adverts. Other types to explore include:

- inserts in printed media;
- messages on appointment cards;
- posters;
- give aways;
- leaflets in counter top dispensers;
- door-to-door leaflets;
- cable television (considerably cheaper than national or terrestrial television and much more focused on particular areas or audiences);
- local radio;
- property hoardings, buses and other transport; and
- the promotional materials of non-competing organisations targeting the same audience.

The Internet is another important advertising medium.

Direct marketing and direct mail

Direct marketing includes any marketing where there is a direct relationship or contact – and therefore includes direct mail, telemarketing or e-marketing (through the Internet, ideally with permission marketing – where someone has given you permission to send them promotional materials electronically over the Internet).

Direct mail is a cost-effective method of reaching commercial clients and referring organisations – as opposed to advertising, which is probably best for reaching private clients. The starting point is some form of database which contains, as well as the name of the individual, their position, the organisation name, the address, the telephone number and their email address. Other useful information would be specific areas of interest (e.g. tax advice, property advice), other relationships or services used within the firm, a list of past contacts and any other information that helps with analysis and segmentation.

Short, simple letters following the AIDA rule (Attention, Interest, Desire and Action) are often effective – especially when the follow-up action is low commitment (e.g. sending in for an information pack, requesting a copy of a helpful checklist, e-mailing a request, visiting a website etc.) rather than high commitment (e.g. a meeting). A covering letter will increase the chances of any brochure or newsletters being read. You should also look at ways to facilitate an easy response such as reply-paid envelopes, freephone telephone numbers or proforma fax sheets. Many firms now offer websites with further information and some have invested in setting up modest call centres to manage enquiries.

Be creative in thinking what you might send to people that will be of value – items should be focused on specific messages or issues. Copies of articles or of speeches you have delivered, feedback or testimonials from clients facing similar situations, invitations to informal briefings or receptions, notification of books or speeches your professional staff have prepared could all be used.

Although there has been a tendency for professional firms to produce high quality, glossy promotional materials, direct mail will work just as well (sometimes even better) if the materials are produced smartly and inexpensively in-house. Such items can often feel more immediate and personal than their glossy counterparts. They can also be tailored to specific needs, topical issues or special audiences with ease.

Direct mail can be used to communicate on a regular basis with existing clients and referrers as well – helping to build relationships, provide added-value service and keep your firm's name 'front of mind'. This is particularly cost-effective and easy to do if you employ an email alert system.

You should be aware that many professional associations have recently changed their rules with regards to cold-calling. This was previously banned. However, some rules still exist to prevent you cold-calling private clients and if you do use this method make sure you are aware of the rules surrounding Data Protection and privacy (e.g. Telephone Preference Services etc).

Public relations (including media relations)

This is a broad term which covers a whole range of activities involving the firm in two-way communications with the various publics it serves. Relevant publics for professional firms might include existing clients of the particular service being promoted, other existing clients of the firm, potential clients, local referrers, the local media, existing staff, potential staff, other professions, the banking and finance community and government officials.

MEDIA RELATIONS

Media relations (i.e. structured communication with printed and broadcast media) is one of the most useful tools for professional firms. Timely press releases about topical issues, offering the expert views of your leading professionals, short articles providing practical advice, articles containing checklists to help readers assess their situation and 'advice columns', briefings with editors and journalists are all inexpensive (but time intensive) ways of getting your message across. You might scan the main newspapers and be ready to provide comments and advice when a high profile related case or situation hits the headlines. However, unlike advertising, the editor will always have the final say on whether your items are used and the manner in which the material is presented so you have much less control. Unless you have some experience of dealing with the media it is often useful to employ the services of someone who does – freelance journalists or press officers can be used on an occasional basis and their rates are often very reasonable. If you choose wisely you will find a media relations specialist with good knowledge of, and contacts within, the media you have targeted.

PUBLICATIONS

This is another aspect of marketing that falls broadly into public relations too. You might have a firm brochure, a commercial or private client brochure, leaflets describing the services offered by your team or in-depth booklets providing detailed guidance and advice. Again, the key words here are focus and benefits. Too many professionals' publications focus on 'we' the firm rather than 'you' the client and contain features rather than benefits. Truly client-facing publications will be written from the clients' point of view (e.g. problems, needs, questions, concerns, issues, etc.) rather than the firm's point of view (location, departments, services, etc.). Newsletters will serve a number of purposes. Whether they are general and aimed at all clients or focused on the needs of particular groups they will:

- alert readers to changes in the law or regulations;
- educate them on possible needs they might have;
- provide simple advice so that they can help themselves;
- explain difficult and complex issues or situations in simple terms;
- provide a mechanism by which clients can help themselves;
- remind them that the firm is proactive and able to assist;
- cross-sell services of the firm;
- secure the loyalty and memory of existing or dormant clients.

In these Internet days it is important to remember that many client groups prefer to receive or access information on-line. So consider the extent to which your publications are available on-line. A short email including a link to more indepth information on a particular area of your website might be a more effective way to alert clients and potential clients to information of value. Some firms have invested in the production of short and interesting videos or CD-Roms to convey their message – an interesting alternative to the usual brochure.

EVENTS

Events for existing or potential clients or referrers would also fall under the public relations umbrella. Some firms take exhibition or stand space at specialist trade or local county shows – an opportunity to meet, face-to-face, local people who might be clients or potential clients. Research shows that seminars, training courses and workshops are highly valued by commercial clients and referrers (see below). Corporate hospitality might also be a part of this activity and many professional firms will arrange cocktail parties and Christmas and summer events for their clients and referrers. Some events might be linked to sponsorship arrangements.

SPEAKERS

You might also provide 'expert' speakers to address the audiences of local business, trade, professional, social or special interest groups. Organisations such as the Institute of Directors, the Chambers of Commerce and Business Links are often heavily targeted by other professionals, so seek out more unusual organisations. Similarly, you might send representatives of the firm out to network at these events – the aim being both to develop contacts that might generate or refer business in the future, and also to gather vital information or market intelligence about local needs and competitors, and to ensure that the firm's name appears regularly at local events.

Internal marketing

This area of public relations – communicating with those within your firm – is vitally important because often other members of the firm will be an important source of referrals for you and because sometimes you may be targeting similar audiences to them.

In smaller firms it is easier to talk informally to the partners, assistants, trainees and secretaries within other departments without having to arrange special meetings or prepare lists of the services provided, the clients served and ways in which you can help each other develop business.

Internal marketing is important because you have limited resources within your team and also because very often you will be targeting clients of other parts of the firm. However, the marketing and communication load can be significantly spread if all members of your firm understand what you are offering, to whom, the relative benefits and how to 'pass across' clients or referrers with the sorts of questions or problems that your team can deal with.

Organising seminars, events and networking

These again are aspects of public relations. You might consider planning your marketing on the basis of events that your firm will organise and those that others will organise but your firm will attend.

Organising events can take a huge amount of time and preparation. You will need to call upon your support staff to assist with preparing invitation lists, monitoring the response and the myriad of logistical arrangements (e.g. room preparations, catering, cloakrooms, handouts, audio visual materials, etc.).

At the most informed level, you might invite a selection of clients, potential clients or referrers to your office for lunch or a glass of wine. This provides them with an opportunity to network with other people.

However, many people are invited to 'plain' cocktail parties and receptions so it will help considerably if you can think of something that will make your event different – for example, by having an external guest of honour or by themeing the event in some way.

The events taking most effort are where you are presenting or showcasing your business and/or professional expertise – a briefing for local businesses with a particular planning issue, for local employers with large staffs, for high net worth individuals on future planning etc. Inviting external speakers to your events will both increase the attractiveness to your invitees and reduce the burden on your staff of preparing materials.

Networking can be used to achieve a number of objectives and can be done at your own and other people's events. For example, you can raise the profile of the firm in the local business community or amongst a particular audience (e.g. local social services people or local GPs). You can make introductions and start to establish personal relationships with referrers or potential clients. Networking may also be used to help develop your understanding of the needs, interests and motivations of your target audience.

Talking to people (and listening carefully to what they say) – especially potential clients – is one of the best ways to gather market intelligence. Regular attendance at the same organisation's meetings or events will increase your chances of being recognised and establishing ongoing contacts. Offering to present topical subjects or to explain complicated professional issues with a wide appeal in a simple way – and getting yourself on their speaker's platforms – will help to raise your profile. People at the events will then feel a little easier about approaching you.

PRESENTATIONS

A presentation to a group of existing or potential clients or on a one-to-one basis is a common approach used in marketing and selling situations. These can be formal (where you make a presentation, perhaps using audio-visuals and taking along a team) or informal (where you simply arrange to talk about the clients' organisation or needs and how you have helped clients in similar situations).

Yet not everyone is comfortable making presentations and some professional people have little experience. It is helpful to prepare audio visual materials (whether these be pre-written sheets to talk against, overhead projector slides or PC-based presentations) to guide the speaker and provide additional interest for the audience. Advance planning and rehearsals are vitally important if the quality of your talk is not to undermine your professional skills. Summaries of talks should always be distributed – with your name, the firm's name and contact details marked discretely but clearly on each separate sheet.

Process and physical appearance

These are two aspects of the service you provide that will have an impact on your marketing effectiveness.

Physical evidence covers a number of things including the appearance of your offices and meeting rooms, the appearance and behaviour of your professional and support staff, the style and layout of your marketing materials and correspondence, and even the type of cups you use to serve tea and coffee. As mentioned above, clients are rarely able to determine the quality of the professional advice they receive and will therefore make assumptions about the quality of advice on the basis of those more tangible things they can observe.

Process brings us back to the product element of the marketing mix. Here you need to be concerned with aspects of work management, project control, use of databases and other information sources, productivity aids, electronic sources, expert systems and other 'technologies' that may assist in the production, management and delivery of professional work. We know that price is often driven by costs in professional firms (how many hours to do this or do that) rather than by the value perceived by the client. Reducing the time and level of skilled staff involved in processing the work will reduce the cost and increase the profitability margin.

But process is not simply a 'behind the scenes' production issue. Your process should be designed to maximise client perception and value – through regular communication, keeping them up-to-date with progress, showing exactly what work has been completed, and providing copies of key documents. Too often, clients are unhappy with bills because either they were not informed of progress or they were unaware of just how much work the professional has undertaken for them.

Implementing your plan

Developing an action plan

You have established your objectives and overall marketing strategy and the sections above should have provided you with a number of ideas about how to implement a strategy. You now need to prepare a short, clear, task-orientated action plan – assigning the names of the responsible individuals and the target dates by which the tasks will be completed.

The action plan will achieve a number of things:

- Ensure you select those activities which will help you achieve your objectives.
- Ensure you assign priorities to those actions.
- Ensure you are realistic about what can be achieved with the human and financial resources that you have available.
- Communicate to everyone in the team (and in the wider firm) exactly what is planned and their role and responsibilities.
- Help you monitor progress.

Agreeing a budget

The main cost in marketing most professional services will be the time of the professionals involved in the marketing. Firms often budget out-of-pocket marketing expenditure very carefully but fail even to think about how much time will be used and whether sufficient return on that time investment will be achieved.

Therefore, you need to prepare your budget in two parts. The first is the out-of-pocket expenditure and should cover items such as advertising (especially directory entries), postage for mailings, catering for events, website development, membership and attendance of local events, the cost of entertaining people at lunches and dinners, the production of marketing materials such as leaflets and presentation aids (although many of these can be produced in-house at no cost by using advanced word-processing or desktop publishing facilities) and sponsorships.

As a rule of thumb, professional firms should spend between 1 per cent and 4 per cent of their gross annual fee income on marketing and business development. Consider the overall fee income of the team and think about what proportion you should spend on marketing. Remember that if you have done little or no marketing in the past, you will probably need a little more cash to get you started in the first year than in subsequent years.

The second and more important part of your budget is agreeing how much time each fee earner and support person will spend on marketing each week or each month. The action list – having broken the various marketing activities down into their component tasks – should help with the estimating.

Alternatively, you can allocate a specific amount of time each week or month for each fee earner to spend on marketing and selling. You may need to adjust your time recording system to capture and report on non-chargeable time spent on marketing. One of the main reasons why professional staff do not do marketing is because they feel they only receive recognition and reward for chargeable time (see Chapter nine on Firm-wide issues).

Monitoring the results

After an initial burst of enthusiasm, many professional firms' marketing initiatives flounder and fade away. This is often because there are no mechanisms for:

- monitoring what is happening (and taking action to ensure that it does); and
- feeding back the results and success stories to keep motivation high.

You need to monitor two parts of your marketing – the process and the results. In the early days there may be few results (it is likely to take a few months before any results materialise) so you must monitor the process. You can use the action plan to tick off what actions have been completed. You can review the amount of non-chargeable time being spent by various fee-earners. You can count how many events are attended, how many mailings are issued, how many press releases or articles are produced and so on.

Monitoring the results may require some changes to your internal systems. You need to be able to monitor additional work from existing clients or referrers, and to pinpoint enquiries and work as a direct result of each marketing activity. Logging calls, enquiries, meetings, instructions, income or the amount of press coverage, are all valid ways to measure the success of marketing.

However, at the end of the day the only true measure will be whether the marketing activity delivers the objectives which you set at the beginning of your planning process. That is why it is so important that you spend time ensuring that the objectives are clear and measurable at the outset.

The marketing planning process is summarised below:

STEP 1: ANALYSING YOUR PRESENT SITUATION
- current work, clients and sources;
- skills, staff and services;
- the market;
- pulling your analysis together.

STEP 2: DECIDING WHAT YOU WANT TO ACHIEVE
- setting objectives;
- selecting targets.

STEP 3: AGREEING A STRATEGY
- position in the market;
- packaging the product and the people;
- pricing;
- promotions and internal marketing;
- process and physical evidence.

STEP 4: IMPLEMENTING YOUR PLAN
- developing an action plan;
- agreeing a budget;
- monitoring the results.

A more detailed version of this process – for the marketing professionals – is as follows:

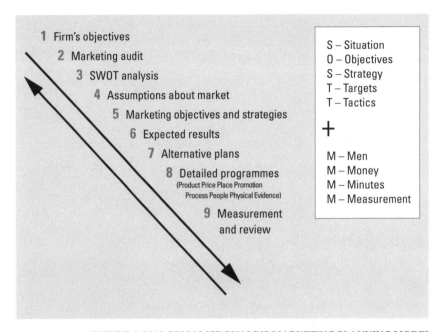

FIGURE 4: MALCOLM MCDONALD'S MARKETING PLANNING MODEL

THREE
What is selling?

ROADMAP

This chapter defines selling and examines the attributes of a good salesperson. There is a review of why selling is different for the professions and the key differences between selling to individuals (private clients – B2C) and organisations (commercial or public sector clients – B2B) are analysed.

Definitions

Marketing, selling and account development are related processes (see Figure 2, page 9). Marketing is concerned with identifying needs in a market, identifying or developing the services that meet those needs and communicating the appropriate messages to the market. It is where the firm 'broadcasts' a message to many members of a market and promotes and builds a brand or proposition. If marketing is successful, enquiries will be generated. Chapter two provides an introduction to marketing and guidance on producing a marketing plan.

When you move from communicating with a market to communicating with a particular organisation or individual you have moved into the selling phase. Here the focus is on the specific needs of that one organisation or individual rather than the generalised needs of the whole market.

The continued marketing and selling to that client to ensure further instructions are received for additional or new services – is a vital activity in every professional firm.

The definition of SELL

To give or give up for money; to betray; to impose upon; trick; to promote the sale of; to make acceptable; to cause someone to accept (e.g. an idea, plan); to convince (someone) of the value of something; to praise; to cry up.

CHAMBERS DICTIONARY

Selling is not a particularly attractive word, which may explain some of the distaste felt by professionals towards it. However, most definitions imply 'exchange' – usually of money – with both sides to the transaction benefiting or receiving what they want.

It implies that there is a seller and a buyer involved in an active process. When professionals are involved in commercial clients, the sale is often described as 'complex' because often more than one individual is involved in the buying process and the selling process (sales cycle) can be protracted.

What makes a good salesperson?

This is a bit like asking what makes a good lawyer, accountant or surveyor – there are many different types and styles, none of which is 'best'. Clearly, the particular client and selling situation requires different skills, personalities and techniques. Recent discussions with professional people indicate the following skills are most important:

- Listening
- Researching
- Confidence
- Planning
- Presenting
- Integrity
- Empathy
- Likes people
- Resilience
- Talking
- Creativity

- Determination
- Negotiating
- Consistency
- Social skills
  - personable
  - appearance
  - interest
  - product knowledge
  - good manners
  - business acumen
  - patience
  - understanding)
  - sincerity

 Positive thinking. Persistence. Present benefits. Passion.
KEITH STEVENSON (GO SELLING)

However, I guess we would all agree that a good salesperson is one where the buyer ends up with what they want at an appropriate price and feeling like the salesperson has done a good – perhaps even transparent – job. A key element that often comes up is the issue of trust. Here, post-purchase satisfaction rears its head. Feeling good during the selling/buying process must continue afterwards if we are to judge someone as a good salesperson. Post-purchase satisfaction is essential for a professional firm otherwise the chances of developing the relationship are minimal.

Why is selling different for the professions?

There are many reasons why selling is different for professionals:

Services not products

First, a professional person is selling an intangible service rather than a tangible product. In order to experience the service the buyer must commit to some element of purchase – so trust is a vital issue. Secondly, a professional service has a number of elements – there is the core expertise (in law, accountancy, property, technology etc.) and there is the way that expertise is delivered. Often, the buyer will not be qualified to make a decision as to the quality of the expertise and most research shows that buyers of professional service either take the quality of expertise for granted or infer it on the basis of the quality of delivery. The intangibility of a professional service means that the buyer experiences a high level of uncertainty about what they are buying and what they are likely to receive – therefore there is a high level of risk which means they will need reassurance from, and to trust in, those that they buy from.

Buying people

The quality of the service is based on the quality of the people providing that service. Therefore, in a professional service environment the buyer is trying to assess the quality of the individuals who will deliver that service. In effect, the salesman/woman is the service. Therefore, the professional's style of selling must reflect those professional qualities that the buyer will experience in the professional relationship where the advice is delivered. Most professionals will feel that in order to 'sell themselves' they will need to be immodest.

Fear of failure

The professions are taught not to fail. The professions are not expected to fail. Professional indemnity is there to protect those unfortunate professionals who make mistakes or fail. Most practices are intolerant of failure. Early failures or mistakes in a professional career can have long lasting impact.

It is therefore not surprising that most professionals fear selling because they lack training in selling and also fear ridicule and failure. They see selling as a risky business with regards to their career and their reputation. Yet, it is impossible to win every sale that you seek – therefore, implied in effective selling is the occasional failure. This is an incredibly hard attitudinal and cultural transition to make.

Expert status

Most clients perceive their professional advisers as experts. Experts are expected to know all the answers. The usual style and approach of an expert is not appropriate to selling in new client situations which means that often professionals do not know how to 'shift gear' from expert mode to selling mode (or to integrate the two modes where appropriate) with ease.

Do it all

The professional has to undertake a multiplicity of roles. He or she has to do the marketing, the selling and then actually produce the goods and deliver them to the client as well as supervise the work and organise billing and payment. Each professional must therefore acquire and use a wide range of skills, which in other types of company would be focused in specialist units (e.g. sales, finance, quality control etc.).

Ethics and integrity

Most professions still have professional rules about acting in the best interests of the clients and somehow selling still feels outside of this definition. It is not until you see selling as a vital part of matching the clients needs against the services and advice you can offer, that you start to see how a professional could and should sell.

Training

As marketing and selling are relatively new in the professions (it was only in the 1980s when the professional rules were relaxed for lawyers and accountants) few professionals have received proper sales training as part of their career development. In some respects, it is hoped that they will pick up the appropriate behaviours by observing their seniors and absorbing the correct approaches. This is a bit like expecting someone to learn how to drive by being an observant passenger. It can work but would be quicker, cheaper and less painful if some professional lessons were provided.

Ongoing relationship

Most professionals expect there to be an ongoing relationship with the client. A close and confidential relationship is not conducive to the perceived relative harshness of selling. Many fear that by trying to sell this may detract from or harm the existing client relationship.

Attitude

For many years the prevalent feeling was that if a professional did a good job, their clients would be happy and would recommend them to other clients. During the heyday of professional services when demand outstripped supply, few professionals needed to do anything more than pick up the phone to take the constant stream of new instructions. This attitude prevails in some areas making professionals feel that if they have to sell then they have somehow failed in their professional endeavours.

Transactional

Some professionals (e.g. corporate finance specialists, architects, personal injury and probate litigators etc.) are involved in work of a very transactional nature – where the opportunities to win business are difficult to predict and rare, and where, therefore, the chances of developing an ongoing relationship with the client are minimal. This often requires a marketing and selling approach which is targeted at other intermediaries or carried out in conjunction with professionals in the same firm whose work is more likely to bring them in contact with clients on a day-to-day basis.

What is a professional?

David Maister's important book *True Professionalism* defines a professional as having the following characteristics:

- Studied a body of knowledge.
- Member of a professional body and bound by professional rules.
- Takes pride in their work – a commitment to quality.
- Reaches out for responsibility.
- Anticipates and takes the initiative.
- Does whatever it takes to get the job done.
- Gets involved and does not stick to the assigned role.
- Always looking for ways to make it easier for those they serve.
- Eager to learn as much as they can about the client.
- Really listens to the needs of those they serve.
- Learns to think like and understand those they serve.
- A team player.
- Can be trusted with confidences.
- Honest, trustworthy, loyal and ethical.
- Open to constructive criticism on how to improve.
- Only acts in the client's best interest.

With the possible exception of the first two, I would argue that this is the very list that defines a really good professional salesperson. If you believe this you could save yourself the time and trouble of reading this book and developing selling skills, however, most of you will need a bit more convincing!

Consumer versus Business-to-Business sales

Some professionals have to sell to private individuals (consumers) as opposed to commercial or public sector organisations. Marketing and selling techniques can vary significantly depending on whether the targets are individuals (consumer marketing – Business-to-Consumer, 'B2C') or businesses (Business-to-Business marketing, 'B2B').

Some of the key differences in these two overall segments are as follows and further explanation is provided in Chapter two (p18):

ATTRIBUTE	CONSUMER/ PRIVATE CLIENT	BUSINESS/ COMMERCIAL CLIENT
Target	An individual or family	Someone or people within a business or partnership
Number in the UK	58 million population	1.6 million registered for VAT (i.e. income over c£50,000)
Needs	Diverse	Diverse
Buyer	An individual	Often several individuals
Technical and professional knowledge	Little	Sometimes little and sometimes a lot (if professionally qualified e.g. in-house lawyers)
Purchase frequency of professional services	Rare	Frequent

ATTRIBUTE	CONSUMER/ PRIVATE CLIENT	BUSINESS/ COMMERCIAL CLIENT
Public information available on target	Relatively little	A significant amount
Funding	Private income or insurance (possibly Legal Aid)	The organisation
Emotional involvement	High	Low
Sales cycle	Short	Long
Ongoing relationship	Unlikely/difficult	Desired
Marketing methods	Indirect (e.g. advertising, media relations, intermediaries)	Direct (e.g. direct marketing, personal selling)

FOUR

Adopting the buyer's point of view: An introduction to buyer behaviour and relevant psychology

66 *The deepest principle in human nature is the craving to be appreciated.* 99

WILLIAM JAMES (PSYCHOLOGIST)

ROADMAP

Initially, a number of concepts that are useful in understanding the psychology of individuals (e.g. personality, perception, motivation etc.) are examined as well as some insights into how group dynamics work. Then the most frequently used models of individual buyer behaviour are reviewed including the decision-making process and different buying situations. This chapter is important for all professions as we all have to work with people, but is particularly relevant to those involved in private client situations. The later part goes on to explore some important models of organisational and industrial buying behaviour (particularly the decision-making unit) which will be useful to those working with commercial clients. Some of these concepts are fundamental to understanding Chapter five on commonly taught selling frameworks. At the end, different buying criteria are reviewed.

Introduction

Inevitably, many sales training books and materials start with the provision of a selling framework. This has always seemed to me to be putting the cart before the horse. At the end of the day each buyer is a person and an individual. Each individual has a personality, motivations and beliefs. In a selling situation, the individual has two levels of need – the need they must fulfil in the acquisition of the service they are seeking, in order to overcome the specific problem identified, or to acquire the benefits that they seek. But they also have needs as a person to transact that sale or to buy in a manner that suits their personal needs.

One of the most important issues in any form of marketing and selling – and especially in the professions where there is a tendency to get carried away with the importance of a specialist expert – is to adopt the buyers' point of view and try to understand what the buyer is thinking in both a professional and a personal capacity. Although we all like to think that we make decisions on a rational basis, our emotions and irrational processes play a very important part too.

To try to think and feel like your buyer means that you need to develop empathy with them. There are text books devoted to this empathetic approach to selling – see the book list in Appendix two. There are many different types of buyer (the individual, the family, the small commercial organisation, the large public sector organisation etc.) and there are several models of buyer behaviour and many psychological theories about how people perceive things and what drives their motivation and behaviour. Any further study of human psychology will assist you in the selling process but, for brevity, just a few directly useful models and theories are examined below.

Individuals

It is tempting at this point to provide a comprehensive review of the wide range of psychological models developed to explain these most complex human processes. However, we are limited in space and therefore just a few illustrative models – and how they can help professionals – are reviewed here. Let us start by recognising that there is a multitude of forces at work in any buying situation.

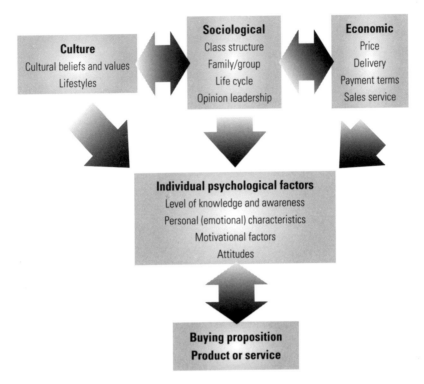

FIGURE 5: COMPLEX PATTERN OF BUYING INFLUENCERS (CHISNALL)

We cannot examine all of the points outlined on the previous page in detail, but some key elements are addressed below.

Personality

Personality is a hugely complex and controversial subject. Psychologists still debate fiercely the value of personality models and there are hundreds to choose from – of varying quality in terms of their scientific integrity. It is important to note too that no model explains real life – they are tools to assist you and no individual will fit exactly into any one category. We are only concerned with the extent to which these models are useful to a professional person in a sales situation – they show us that others are different to ourselves and to support positive interactions we must a) recognise the differences and b) perhaps adapt our thoughts and behaviour to help the other person feel more comfortable with the situation.

Classification of personality types

TRAIT	RANGE OF TYPES
Compulsiveness	Compulsive-Non compulsive
Gregariousness	Extrovert-Introvert
Autonomy	Dependent-Independent
Conservatism	Conservative-Radical
Authoritarianism	Authoritarian-Democratic
Leadership	Leader-Follower
Ambitious	High achiever-Low achiever

Empathy selling personality types

STEREOTYPE	DOMINANT DESIRE
Normal	Social approval
Mover	Communication

Ditherer	Security
Artist	Creativity
Politician	Win
Engineer	Complete projects
Hustler	Material success

Analytical	**Commander**
(Thinking)	(Action)
• Prepare well in advance	• Be brief/to the point
• Be clear and rational	• Avoid chat/social pleasantries
• Avoid emotions	• Stick to the business at hand
• Create action plans	• Mention objectives and results
Amiable	**Expressives**
(Relationships)	(Intuition)
• Take time	• Entertain and stimulate
• Learn background	• Be lively and enthusiastic
• Ask for their opinions	• Ask their opinions
• Reassure them about others	• Remember the big picture
	• Don't get lost in detail

FIGURE 6: TYPES OF MANAGER (DAVID MERRILL)

This is an extension and combination of many other models and is a common base in many sales training courses for professional people. However, it requires the completion of questionnaires to identify your own and your client's dominant mode.

Myers Briggs personality and cognitive traits

Each individual is described on four bipolar scales where the dominant trait is recognised in a descriptor such as ISTJ (which is what most professionals are classified as!):

- Introvert (I) – Extrovert (E)
- Sensory (S) – Intuitive (N)
- Thinking (T) – Feeling (F)
- Judging (J) – Perceiving (P)

To use these models, the professional must first know their dominant type of personality and find a way to quickly assess the personality type of the person they are selling to. This is often not an easy task, for example, it takes the completion of a detailed questionnaire to assess your Myers Briggs profile. Furthermore, people adapt their behaviour in different situations which may appear as if they are modifying their personality.

The concept here is that the seller must adapt their behaviour and approach to 'fit the needs' more precisely of the personality of the buyer. Again, adaptation of your own behaviour is difficult to achieve and many would counsel that you remain 'true to yourself' in all business situations.

However, many people feel that the insights they gain into personality types (and the different behaviours commonly associated with them) helps them greatly when dealing with people who are different to themselves. Some professionals decide that they will actively seek out those clients and potential clients who share a similar personality type to themselves – and call in their colleagues when they must deal with people of a very different personality type.

Enneagram – Nine basic personality types

Another personality model uses nine different personality types:

- Reformer/perfectionist
- Helper/giver
- Motivator/performer
- Individual/tragic romantic
- Investigator/observer
- Loyalist/devil's advocate
- Enthusiast/epicure
- Leader/boss
- Peacemaker/mediator

Again, some professionals find it useful to be able to classify themselves and develop strategies for dealing with people with very different profiles.

Learning styles

If your buyer must learn important new concepts or ideas in order to appreciate the nature of the service they are buying from you then it is useful to know that people acquire knowledge in different ways and have, effectively, different learning styles.

Peter Honey has shown that the manner in which people prefer to learn can be categorised as follows:

Preferred method	Learning style
Experience	Activist
Reflection	Reflector
Conclusions	Theorist
Plan	Pragmatist

In selling situations this is important. For example, an activist will be more comfortable in, for example, a workshop environment trying something out for themselves whereas a theorist will be happier reading through information provided by an expert. Again, the salesperson can alter aspects of the selling process to ensure that the personal needs and style of the buyer are matched.

3D Personalities

Although these personality models have much to offer, my preference is for simple tools that enable people to grasp the essence of the differences between themselves and others and thus adapt their behaviour accordingly. One of my favourite, very simple models, categorises personalities into three broad types:

DOMINANT	Needs to control
	Needs to win
	Will make decisions quickly
DETACHED	Relies on facts and logic
	Dislikes social interaction
	(Note: Most professionals fall into this category!)
DEPENDENT	Needs social approval
	Likes to chat and smile
	Needs a pleasant relationship/interaction
	Will need guidance/direction

Cultural styles

When you are dealing with clients or account teams comprising individuals from different cultures it is important that you understand and adapt to their styles – rather than trying to impose your own cultural style. This is a complex area and you are recommended to take specialist training if this is a major aspect of your role.

A useful model was developed by Hofstede to provide a diagram of the key differences in cultural styles:

- Individualist-Collectivist
- Masculine-Feminine
- Low power distance-High power distance
- Weak uncertainty avoidance-Strong uncertainty avoidance

Emotional intelligence (EQ)

Many people will be familiar with the concept of IQ (Intelligence Quotient) as a measure of how intelligent people are. Recently, people have identified the idea of emotional intelligence as:

The ability to perceive, integrate, understand and reflectively manage one's own feelings and other people's feelings.

JOHN D MAYER AND PETER SALOVEY

EQ is very important within selling. Those who have been shown to have high levels of EQ are much better at selling (and at leading people). Daniel Goleman indicated that there are different aspects of EQ:

1. Know one's emotions (self awareness)
2. Manage one's emotions (handling feelings)

3   Motivate oneself (marshalling emotions in service of a goal)

4   Recognise emotions in others (empathy)

5   Handle relationships (social competence)

Some professionals have found that the study and development of EQ has improved their sales effectiveness significantly.

Perception

We interpret information received through our senses in a unique and individual way. The understanding of human perception is a highly specialist field of psychology and social cognition is the area concerned with perception in social interactions.

Perception is affected by our backgrounds and personality and also our ability to selectively receive only the information which interests us or supports our views. The 'cocktail party' phenomenum demonstrates this – in a busy and noisy room we cannot hear the content of the conversations going on around us, however, we will hear if someone mentions our name or the name of someone to whom we are close. Our interpretation of an event or a person will therefore differ from someone else's interpretation of that same event or person.

I often remind professionals that 'perception is reality'. It does not matter what your firm is or what it does, what matters is how the client perceives your firm. If the client has a very different perception of your firm to the reality then you need to spend time helping them modify their perceptions. In order to do this, you must first explore carefully how your client perceives your firm. Doing this across whole markets is where marketers study how your firm is 'positioned' against its competitors in the minds of the market.

People perception

How people perceive each other is clearly important for those in selling situations. There are thought to be a number of different processes in people perception (Schneider, Hastorf and Ellsworth):

1 **Attention**: The observer will select certain features from their physical appearance, the context and behaviour – and categorise the person.

2 **Snap judgement**: An inference will be made from appearance and behaviour which may include affective reaction (attraction or repulsion) and stereotypic judgements.

3 **Attribution**: Reflective judgements involving more thought.

4 **Trait implication**: Assumptions based on attribution (e.g. This person is arrogant).

5 **Impression formation**: Combining all the traits and organising them to form a coherent impression – and some of the traits that do not fit the overall impression will be disregarded. The primacy effect works here – as those impressions formed earliest have the greatest impact on the overall impression.

6 **Prediction of future behaviour**: With a formed impression, the person will now feel able to predict the behaviour of the person.

For those attempting to sell, there are two clear messages here:

a) Make sure that your appearance and behaviour accurately conveys the sort of impression you want to make.

b) Be aware that initial impressions have a lasting impact.

Motivation

There are lots of motivation theories concerned with instincts, basic needs and drives (e.g. to reduce thirst, to reduce hunger, to reproduce). The Maslow model recognises some of the motivations beyond these basic needs:

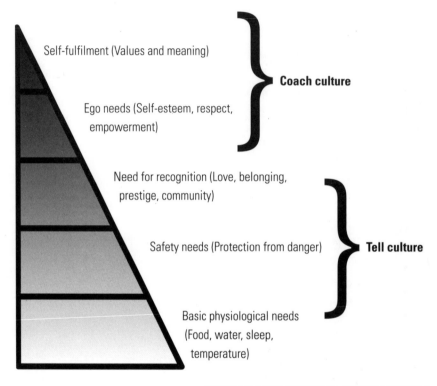

FIGURE 7: MASLOW'S HIERARCHY OF NEEDS

There is one particular element of motivation theory that is important for professional selling. Humans generally have a need to reduce dissonance between conflicting beliefs or conflicting beliefs and actions. Cognitive dissonance theory (Festinger) suggests that when people experience this type of conflict they are motivated to alter their beliefs or actions to become more consistent.

For example, if they have taken great effort to select their present advisers, pay them reasonable fees and the service they receive is not very good, one of two things will happen. The rational response would be to change their advisers to get some who provide a good service. However, a frequent response is to either convince yourself that you ARE getting good service or decide that it is your fault (e.g. 'I am a demanding client') that the service is not delivered well.

Curiosity is one of the basic human motivations. It can help secure an initial meeting or get attention at the beginning of a communication or presentation.

Motivation is also important when you are trying to promote a selling culture within your firm – see Chapter nine on Firm-wide issues. The following may also help:

ENSURING MOTIVATION (HERZBERG)

**Hygiene factors =
Satisfy basic needs:**

- Salary and benefits
- Working conditions
- Company policy
- Status
- Job Security
- Supervision and autonomy
- Office life
- Personal life

Failure to meet hygiene factors causes dissatisfaction

Motivators:

- Achievement
- Recognition
- Job interest
- Responsibility
- Advancement

Life cycle

For professionals involved in selling to individuals (private clients) it may be helpful to use the life cycle model to adapt their selling activities and approaches as well as in their market segmentation (an important marketing theory see Chapter two):

- Bachelor
- Newly married
- Full nest I (young dependent children)
- Full nest II (older dependent children)
- Empty nest
- Solitary survivor.

The idea here is that people at similar stages of their life cycle will have similar needs and motivations and adopt similar buying behaviours. For example, whereas a bachelor or newly married are unlikely to need a will writing service, it is a common requirement once people enter the full nest stage. Similarly, estate agents will be able to relate differing property needs to differing stages of the life cycle – initially a growing need for space and then a decline in need for space, and perhaps different locational needs.

The decision-making process

Initially, it was thought that buyers progressed through a rational process when making a decision. The following figure is typical:

FIGURE 8: THE DECISION-MAKING PROCESS

Although there are many limitations, the model does provide some guidance to the selling process:

- Sometimes the professional must help the client recognise and define the problem. By focusing on this education process, the professional is more likely to be able to influence the remainder of the process, thus increasing their chances of success with that client. Please refer to the information above about learning styles.

- Where and how will the client search for information? The answer to this question should be the centrepiece of your marketing strategy. However, from a sales perspective, trying to force a decision whilst the client is still learning about and defining the problem is likely to end in failure. Similarly, helping a client obtain the information they seek (and providing additional information that will enhance their decision-making ability) will enhance your progress in subsequent stages.

- If you enter the process when the client is evaluating alternatives, they will have already established the criteria against which they are evaluating different solutions. Your task is to understand what those criteria are if you are to be successful. Typically, clients are at this stage when they issue a competitive tender (see Chapter seven).

A later version of this model has a number of additional phases:

- Problem identification
- Problem definition
- Solution specification
- Search
- Assessment
- Selection
- Agreement
- Monitor.

More recently, consumer models have indicated that buying behaviour is affected by many other influences such as mood and occasion, and that very different processes can operate depending on these factors.

Group dynamics

How individuals work together in groups is important for the professions in two respects – first, often commercial clients will operate in groups when selecting, assessing or working with their professional advisers and second, often in marketing and selling professional services you will need your fee-earners to operate in teams – either to tender for new business or in the context of a major client or account management team.

Social and occupational psychology are large areas and your Human Resources personnel should be able to help you further. However, some of the most common and most valuable ideas for the professions in selling situations are shown below:

Belbin developed a model to consider the different roles adopted by team members and showed the importance of having the right mix of 'types':

- Shaper
- Chairperson
- Plant
- Resource instigator
- Monitor evaluator
- Team worker
- Company worker
- Completer finisher

Another important concept is that of Janis around 'Group Think' – this is where a team has developed such a close working bond that they tend to adopt a very similar attitude to situations regardless of what the evidence may suggest. A common issue for groups of partners!

When putting together a new team or group, you should be aware that they may go through a number of processes before they reach a satisfactory level of performance:

- Forming (inclusion)
- Storming (assertion)
- Norming (co-operation)
- Performing

Buying situations

Although some decisions can be made more or less spontaneously, most purchases of professional services are unlikely to be so. Some models point to the different problem solving behaviour depending on the nature of the purchase:

- **Routine problem solving**: when buying consumer or low value goods, little information is needed and price and risk are low. The decision is taken in a quick and routine way.

- **Limited problem solving**: when buying a new or unfamiliar brand or a slightly more expensive item.

- **Extensive problem solving**: this requires a more detailed search for information and evaluation of alternatives where the purchase is very high value and/or relatively rare or there is a high degree of personal commitment (e.g. time).

Most professional services clients will engage in some information seeking and evaluation of alternatives.

An additional issue is to consider the different types of buying situations (Robinson, Faris and Wind).

- **New task**: Purchasing something for the first time. For example, an individual first purchasing advice to write a will or a firm first appointing advisers to assist in a flotation.

- **Modified rebuy**: Changing the nature of the service or supplier. This might be where an individual selects a different solicitor to do the conveyancing on their second or third home. It might be a firm purchasing tax advice from its auditors for the first time.

- **Routine rebuy**: Regular purchases of the same service. This might be where an individual asks their accountant to prepare another tax return or a retailer instructs its surveyors to find yet another outlet.

Again, the professional must be prepared to adjust their sales approach significantly depending on which type of purchase situation is apparent.

Organisational buying behaviour

When selling to organisations (commercial or public sector clients) you are involved in a complex sale and not only must you take account of all the ideas and information about individual buyers but you must also recognise that there are different behaviours that result from these people interacting in a business context. It means that there is no 'one approach fits all' to selling to organisations but that your sales strategy and approach must be designed for each decision-making unit – and sometimes this may change within the same organisation for different buying decisions.

Decision-making unit

In commercial or business-to-business selling situations we have to deal with a multiplicity of potential buyers. Each of the people in an organisation involved in reaching the purchase decision will have a different professional and personal role. One of the classic models (Bonamar) for considering organisational buying behaviour is the decision-making unit:

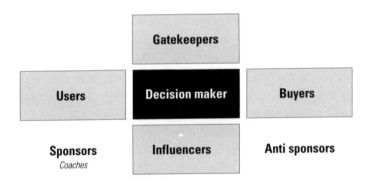

FIGURE 9: THE DECISION-MAKING UNIT

This model is vital for those with commercial clients as they have to identify the different people in the various roles (there can be various people fulfilling a particular role) and adjust their sales approach to suit their needs.

GATEKEEPERS

Typically, these are receptionists, secretaries and assistants who control access to more senior people and the decision-makers. Sometimes they may be more senior people who are tasked with screening and assessing potential suppliers. By alienating these people (e.g. by failing to show respect) you are making your job much more difficult. Getting these people onside, asking for their help, taking an interest in them, inviting them to meetings, showing respect and recognising the importance of their role could help you gain valuable information and ease your access to the decision-makers. The primary role is one of rapport development. You may have difficulty gaining access to more senior people if your 'entry point' into an organisation has been through a gatekeeper as you will need to avoid to be seen 'going over their heads'. It is also important to remember that today's gatekeeper may be tomorrow's influencer, user or decision-maker. Using your younger and/or more junior staff to develop relationships with their peers in prospect or client organisations is a proven strategy.

USERS

These are people who are not directly involved in the decision process but who will be using the services purchased centrally. For example, in a legal situation the in-house lawyer may be the main decision-maker but contracts or commercial managers in branch offices may be the main users of the service. Similarly, the finance director may be the final decision-maker with regards to the firm's accountants but all the other directors will have needs that are addressed by the accountants. Often, one or two of the users will take a keen interest in the purchase of professional services and may play a significant role in the decision-making process. The primary role is rapport development, although their needs and expectations must be fully understood as they play a key role in post-purchase evaluation. Although it is not always necessary to win these people over, it is important that these people are not alienated or excluded from the sales process if they demonstrate an interest.

BUYERS

These are people who are qualified to provide a technical specification of the services being purchased. It could be the organisation's purchasing director, an in-house qualified professional or even an external consultant (as happens occasionally when an external consultant oversees a competitive tendering situation). They may maintain the 'roster' or panel of approved professional service suppliers. Your role here is more as an objective, rational, information provider. Typically, buyers will have a specification or series of criteria against which they assess potential suppliers and they may have sophisticated processes and policies. Your task is to provide them with the information they need – in the format and style that they need it – so that you do not fall at one of the early hurdles. Buyers are typically concerned with the buying process, ensuring that the organisation's quality and supplier minimum requirements are met and so they will have a good insight into the decision-making process at the organisation. They are thus useful allies and you gain their support by making their task easier and minimising the amount of work they have to do.

INFLUENCERS

These people often do not have an official role in the decision process but, by merit of the trust bestowed upon them by senior decision-makers, can play an important part. They are difficult to manage in the sales process as they are often difficult to detect. They could be a trusted colleague at another organisation, a spouse at home, another professional adviser or a consultant. The approach you adopt to developing your referrer and intermediary network may help you identify influencers who can play a useful role in opening doors and introducing you as well as 'sponsoring' your cause (or not) within an organisation.

DECISION-MAKERS

These are the individuals who make the final decision. For professional services it could be the chairman, the managing director, a functional director or an in-house professional. One of the most difficult jobs is identifying the ultimate decision-maker as often they will only appear at the end of the sales process, having delegated initial discussions to more junior staff. Some sales approaches call these people the economic decision-maker as once the decision reaches this person they will assume that all the criteria will have been investigated and met, and their focus may be on the price or the non-rational aspects of the purchase decision. It is also important to remember that within an organisation the decision-maker may change depending on the specific decision being made so you must guard against always viewing the same person as the key decision-maker. When selling to these people you must ensure you do not focus on the technical or other details of the situation – these people are generally concerned with the higher level, strategic impacts on the organisation.

SPONSORS AND ANTI-SPONSORS

These are the people in the organisation who either support your firm or are against it. For example, there may be an individual who has used your firm in a previous organisation and is keen to use your services again. Some models call sponsors 'coaches'. An anti-sponsor may be an individual who is reluctant to give up their existing advisers or who is fearful of change. They will use their influence within the organisation to support or hinder your progress. Former employees of your organisation may fall into the sponsor or anti-sponsor category depending on the nature of the relationship when they left your firm.

Industrial purchasing models

There are several models to describe the industrial or commercial buying models in the framework of broader organisational and environmental factors. These models are of limited value to professionals except to alert them to the presence of uncontrollable and wider factors which may affect the buying situation. However, they outline the interaction of personal and organisational issues which need to be managed in the sale of professional services to guard against the initial purchase (usually of one individual from a professional firm) remaining the norm and thus preventing later cross-selling. They can also act as a checklist for the research phase (see Chapter six) of the sales cycle to ensure that all appropriate issues have been explored.

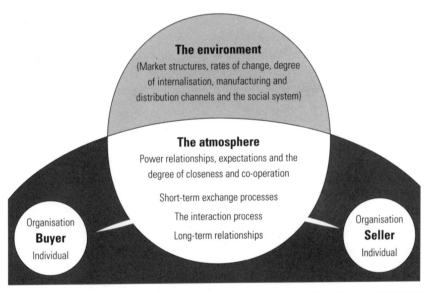

The environment
(Market structures, rates of change, degree of internalisation, manufacturing and distribution channels and the social system)

The atmosphere
Power relationships, expectations and the degree of closeness and co-operation

Short-term exchange processes

The interaction process

Long-term relationships

Organisation
Buyer
Individual

Organisation
Seller
Individual

FIGURE 10: THE INTERACTION MODEL OF INDUSTRIAL MARKETING AND PURCHASING (HAKANSSON)

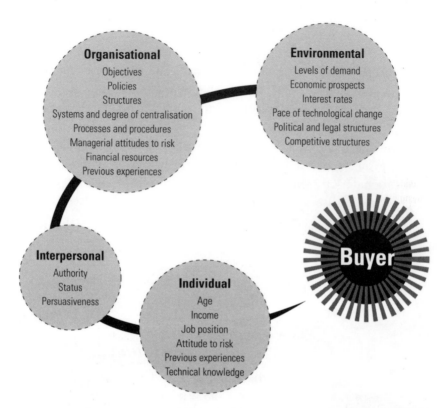

FIGURE 11: FACTORS INFLUENCING INDUSTRIAL BUYING BEHAVIOUR
(WEBSTER AND WIND)

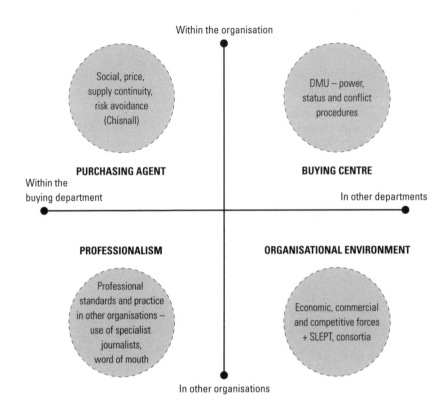

Within the organisation

Social, price,
supply continuity,
risk avoidance
(Chisnall)

DMU – power,
status and conflict
procedures

PURCHASING AGENT

BUYING CENTRE

Within the
buying department

In other departments

PROFESSIONALISM

ORGANISATIONAL ENVIRONMENT

Professional
standards and practice
in other organisations –
use of specialist
journalists,
word of mouth

Economic, commercial
and competitive forces
+ SLEPT, consortia

In other organisations

**FIGURE 12: CONTEXT MODEL FOR ORGANISATION BUYING BEHAVIOUR
(AMERICAN MARKETING ASSOCIATION)**

What these models make clear is that although the relationship between the potential buyer and provider of professional services is very important, and that the nature of the offer is critical, there are often factors beyond this sphere which will impact the decision. Where they are uncontrollable factors the task of the seller is to ensure that they understand them and are prepared to deal with questions relating to the specific sale. Forewarned is forearmed.

These models also remind us that our target clients are focused on the wider organisational, industrial and economic issues affecting their roles – the broader your knowledge of the issues and their organisations and the challenges it faces, the more likely your proposals will strike a chord and differentiate your offer from those of your competitors. Too often the sale of professional services fails as the proposals are too narrow and/or short-term – and fail to take account of their contribution to wider business issues.

Buying criteria

A key element of successful marketing and selling is to put ourselves in our client's shoes – to feel real empathy. Think for a moment how they might feel about purchasing an intangible professional service that they do not understand:

- Intangible (I can't try before I buy).

- A necessary evil (I don't want it but I need it).

- Mysterious and complicated (I don't understand it).

- A means to an end (I just want to buy the property).

- The same regardless of the firm (All advisers are the same).

- Only as good as the adviser involved (I don't like the rest, but Smith is OK).

- Daunting (Those guys and gals are pretty smart).

- Difficult to assess (Which one knows the most and will do the best job?).

- Risky (What if I choose the wrong adviser?).

Before ending the section on buyer behaviour, it is perhaps worth thinking about the criteria that clients use to assess the professional service they are about to purchase. These criteria, to some extent, will depend on some of the internal conversations they are having with themselves about the problem situation. So you must assess the likely buying criteria for each individual in each buying situation.

There have been many private research studies by professional firms and the results are therefore not in the public domain. However, most research studies show that the buyers will attach differing levels of importance to a combination of the following factors:

CRITERIA	EXAMPLE	RELEVANT ISSUES
Security	Everyone knows these advisers	Reputation. Size. Market share
Performance	They have won lots of cases	Track record. Profile
Appearance	They have nice looking offices	Premises. Individual presentation. Corporate identity
Convenience	Just around the corner	Location. Web delivery
Economy	They are the cheapest	Price
Loyalty	I have always used them	Relationship management. Individuals. Satisfaction
Expertise	Good at XYZ	Individuals. Reputation. Profile
Status	The best	Reputation. Price
Durability	Been around for years	History. Stability. Staff turnover and/or continuity
Friendship	I like Jackson a lot	Relationships. Individuals
Accessibility	Always speak to them when I want	Infrastructure. Support services. Fee earner attitude and workload
Reliability	Always respond in an hour	Culture. Infrastructure. Systems. Quality and relationship systems
Reduction of uncertainty	Done OK in the past	Track record. Existing relationship

FIGURE 13: CRITERIA USED TO ASSESS PROFESSIONAL SERVICES

Recent studies have shown that the most important factors in choosing professional advisers include factors such as understanding professional advice requirements in a commercial context, track record and expertise, personal chemistry, innovating new approaches to old problems (better, faster, cheaper etc.) and price. These are somewhat different to the factors used when assessing the ongoing performance of a professional firm (part of the post-purchase satisfaction assessment) which are shown to include: ability to work with your team, responsiveness/speed, interpreting needs in a commercial context, proactive action and ideas and accessibility (partners and other staff).

An important issue will always, of course, be price. However, the absolute price is rarely the key issue. What can make or break a sale is the perceived value of what is being purchased. Also, how your price compares with that of your competitors. In some highly strategic and risky decisions, buyers may wish to buy one of the most expensive solutions as a sort of reassurance that they have done everything they can to secure the best advisers. In these situations a low or competitive price may signal a lack of quality or confidence in the supplier and undermine a successful sales strategy. This is the mixture of financial and emotional value involved in the buying decision. Perceived value will therefore be different for each buyer in each purchase situation and will result in decisions that do not appear logical or rational to the salesperson. Depending on whether there is a high or low perceived value can alter the selling strategy or approach that you adopt.

FIVE

Selling frameworks and models

> You'll have more fun and success when you stop trying to get what you want and start helping other people get what they want.
>
> **DALE CARNEGIE**

ROADMAP

This chapter provides a review of the most common selling frameworks, starting with the older and more traditional models from where we obtained terms such as objections and closing (which are discussed further in Chapter six on Selling skills). It continues with a review of the core ideas in the more recent process or consultative models (that are more suited to the professions) such as Maister, SPIN®, Strategic Selling®, complex selling RADAR™ and behavioural science systems which often form the basis of commercial sales training courses.

Introducing the sales cycle

Selling professional services can be a lengthy process. The sales cycle (i.e. the time from initial contact to winning some work) can vary significantly. In professional services, the sales cycle spans from relatively quick (e.g. a few days between telephoning a solicitor and appointing them to take action on making your will) to extremely long (e.g. several years whilst a commercial organisation decides to appoint your firm as its auditors).

Research has indicated that, in commercial situations, it takes on average eight separate contact points and an average of 18 months to win work from a new client. So professionals who get frustrated when they don't win business straightaway can relax!

Illustration of possible range of contacts during a commercial client sales cycle

- Take a long term view and plan accordingly
- Have realistic expectations
- Not so different from a courtship – gradual development of mutual understanding and trust
- From general to specific interests to specific current need

- Meet for first time (at a networking event)
- Send information (general about the firm)
- Invite to a group event
- Send information (specific interest area)
- Meet or have lunch with others
- Send information (specific and topical issue)
- Invite to a joint hospitality event
- Send a proposal (very specific on particular need)
- Meeting/lunch

It is also important that you consider the importance of selling more work to existing clients which is faster and more cost effective to build your firm in the short-term. Chapter eight on Account management helps with strategies for developing more work from existing clients.

To help sales people to adopt a more structured approach to managing the sales cycle (some refer to this as the sales funnel – see the client relationship ladder figure in Chapter one) and moving it closer to getting the business, many frameworks have been developed. The 'classical' or stage models are probably what most people are familiar with and these models have given us much of our selling terminology with words such as 'objection' and 'close'. However, more recent models use a more needs driven and consultative approach which is generally more appropriate for professional firms.

Classical models

PHASE ONE

- Preparation
- Identify the buyer
- Learn about the buyer
- Identify a need or problem and explore it

PHASE TWO

- Identify the relevant service/solution
- Demonstrate you can solve the problem
- Confirm that the funds (and authority) are available

PHASE THREE

- Decide why now is the time to buy
- Overcome any objections
- Close the sale
- Deliver the promise (and exceed expectations)

FIGURE 14: TRADITIONAL OR 'CLASSICAL' MODEL OF THE SALES PROCESS

This model and its many variants assume that you have completed quite a lot of research and preparation work and are already in contact with someone at the organisation!

Phase one starts with identifying the buyer. This is not always as straightforward as it may appear. It may take you some time to learn that your contact is not the actual buyer (see the decision-making unit in Chapter four) and even more time to identify and make contact with the correct decision-maker. There is then an implied research and rapport building stage where you learn about the buyer – both in their work capacity and as an individual. You should then identify a need – for without an implicit or explicit need there is little point in proceeding. This is often where many professionals spend a long time going nowhere. They cannot see an obvious need for their particular service and are unable to explore whether there might be other needs that are relevant to their colleagues. It may also be necessary to invest time and energy in helping the client to recognise a need. Sales training should concentrate on the appropriate skills and techniques (research, questioning and probing, problem finding etc.) to uncover a need. The SPIN® model focuses almost exclusively on this aspect of the sales process.

Phase two starts with the matching process where, having found a need, you identify which package of services from your firm will meet those needs. It is rare that the solutions you have available match precisely what the client needs. Forcing your solution onto the client's problem is unlikely to be successful. You MUST focus on what the client wants and needs – not what you can most easily provide. A lack of lateral thought here can be an issue. A lack of integrity can result in the firm proposing solutions which do not really address the client's real needs (but serve the needs of the person selling to 'win new business'). However, a failure to properly match needs and solutions at this stage will make the remainder of the selling process difficult and may result in a dissatisfied client and no future business.

To demonstrate you can solve the problem, you need to persuade the client that you have the relevant skills and expertise. Some professionals may draw on case studies of past work or testimonials from other clients. Where trying to sell a new service this can be more difficult as there is no prior track record to lean on. In these situations you are asking the client to take an awful lot on trust – both as a firm and as an individual – and there is a large amount of risk involved for the buyer. It is therefore preferable to only sell new services to existing clients and focus on promoting existing services to new clients (this issue should have been addressed as part of your marketing strategy – which services to be sold into which market – see Chapter two). In this framework you are then required to ensure that funds are available to pay for the services although I would strongly recommend that this is something that is checked right at the outset.

Phase three addresses a common problem for professionals. The client has indicated a need and has accepted that your firm would do an excellent job but they fail to make the decision to confirm the instructions, so you reach an impasse. There are many techniques – some of which are not suitable for professionals – to address this issue which are covered in the next chapter. I would recommend, however, that during phase one you should have identified the reasons for a timely decision. Some of the techniques in the RADAR™ approach are focused on persuading the client that now is the time to make a decision and proceed with the sale.

Closing the sale (see Chapter six) requires asking the client for the business. Again, if a more consultative process has been followed this should follow automatically and naturally without having an uncomfortable question. Delivering the promise is sometimes overlooked as in the excitement of winning the business the professional fails to ensure that the service is delivered according to the client's expectations and the client is then quickly lost.

Skills and techniques to help you at each stage of this process are covered in Chapter six. Through experience I have learnt how this model can be adapted to fit more comfortably within a professional environment (see over):

RESEARCH AND PREPARE:

- Knowledge about your own firm
- Knowledge of the client organisation and industry
- Knowledge of the client's existing advisers
- Knowledge of the individuals making the purchase decision
- Initial ideas about likely needs
- Knowledge and ideas about how your firm could respond to these needs

ESTABLISH CONTACT AND BUILD EMPATHY:

- Persuade the client to allocate time to meet
- Provide an agenda
- Decide in advance what you hope to achieve
- Demonstrate an interest in the individual
- Concentrate on developing empathy and rapport
- Clarify the decision-making process at the client's organisation

EXPLORE NEEDS:

- Ask relevant questions
- Confirm your understanding of the issues
- Offer ideas and suggestions to gauge reaction
- Provide a reason to sustain the information exchange
- Identify any potential issues or constraints

AGREE THE NEXT STEPS

COMPLETE THE FOLLOW UP ACTIONS

FIGURE 15: MODIFIED APPROACH TO THE CLASSICAL SALES PROCESS

(© KIM TASSO 2000)

You will notice that this suggests an interactive process that is repeated, to some extent, at each contact point and does not indicate exactly where the process will end. This is because in professional services some sales cycles are short and some are protracted, so offering a series of activities that must be repeated as necessary is more appropriate. You might also need to repeat the process with each member of the decision-making process at the buying organisation.

Consultative or process models

Most professionals are more comfortable with what are called 'consultative' or 'process driven' models. In these models selling is replaced by a problem-solving approach which is more focused on the need for the client to find a solution, than the professional's need to sell.

Maister

David Maister is a lawyer who has written many books on managing law firms and professional practices. He is now a professor at Harvard Business School and often-quoted and highly respected on a wide range of issues for professional firms and management of modern enterprises. His book *True Professionalism* should be required reading for all professionals and many larger management consultancies insist that their new recruits do so. Although I am a self professed fan of David Maister and agree whole-heartedly with his overall approach to management in professional firms, I have found his model of business development to be somewhat lacking in assistance when it comes to practical application in business development for the majority of professionals. However, it serves as a good model for many professionals:

Broadcasting – Marketing

Courting – Selling

Superpleasing – Quality and account/client development

Nurturing

Listening

FIGURE 16: MAISTER'S MODEL OF BUSINESS DEVELOPMENT

Ask your clients how you can serve them better

Invest heavily in your existing clients by demonstrating
an interest in their affairs

Decide which new clients you would be willing to serve free

Design a package of activities to demonstrate that you have
a special interest in the prospective client

Forget about talking about yourself and your company – the key is listening
and your abilities to find out what the clients want

FIGURE 17: MAISTER'S MODEL

His model highlights some very important concepts: the need to listen, the need to continue to develop existing client relations and the need to identify 'dream' clients (see targeting in Chapter six). It is particularly suitable to firms where there is no formal marketing plan and where the partners are used to developing their own distinct practice areas, without much involvement from their colleagues elsewhere in the firm. So if there is little 'corporate' spirit at your firm his models will help individual professionals who are faced with developing their practice areas alone.

The SPIN® Selling Skills model

Huthwaite Research Group under Neil Rackman, a research psychologist, analysed more than 35,000 sales calls over a period of 12 years. The focus of the research was the use of open and closed questions (see Chapter six on Selling skills) in complex sales situations. The result was the SPIN® approach to complex sales, which is one of the leading sales training frameworks in the world. It provides a consultative and diagnostic approach to selling situations so that the problem becomes clearer and more significant and thus paves the way for acceptance of a proposed solution and its benefits. Professionals who are involved in commercial or public sector clients will find much value in the approach – although attendance at a SPIN® training course is recommended.

The approach describes the four stages of the sales call:

1   preliminaries;
2   investigating;
3   demonstrating capability; and
4   obtaining commitment

and provides advice and guidance for each. SPIN® describes the types and order of questions (Situation, Problem, Implication and Need-payoff) to be asked during the investigating stage to convert Implied Needs into Explicit Needs.

It addresses the common problem for many professionals of the prospective client agreeing to further contact without getting any nearer the prospect of a sale (a continuance being ongoing contact, whereas an advance gets closer to a sale) and provides strategies for dealing with such situations.

Further information about SPIN® can be obtained from Huthwaite International (telephone: 01709 710081, website: www.huthwaite.co.uk).

Strategic selling®

This approach was developed and recently refined by Miller Heiman. Although it is the basis of an intensive sales training programme there are many elements which can be considered separately. Overall, it is based on the decision-making unit concepts mentioned earlier (see Chapter four). They define a complex sale as 'one in which a number of people give their approval or input before a buying decision can be made'. The approach is based on these premises:

- **Premise 1**: Whatever got you where you are today is no longer sufficient to keep you there.

- **Premise 2**: In the complex sale, a good tactical plan is only as good as the strategy that led up to it. The approach provides a series of questions to help you work on your strategy:

    1   Analyse your current position with regard to the client and your objectives.

    2   Think through possible alternate positions.

    3   Determine which alternate position would best secure your objective and devise an action plan to achieve it.

    4   Implement your action plan (i.e. the tactics).

- **Premise 3**: You can succeed in sales today only if you know what you are doing and why.

Strategic selling® separates selling into two distinct components – strategic and tactical. The strategic element is closely aligned with marketing thinking in that it is concerned with getting yourself in the right place with the right people at the right time (see Chapter two). Inherently, it takes an account planning approach (see Chapter eight on Account management).

Strategic selling® then goes on to describe in some detail six key elements of a sale:

1 BUYING INFLUENCES

This relates closely to the decision-making unit (DMU) model examined in Chapter four. It requires you to identify those people in the various roles and the specific economic buying influencer (decision-maker in the DMU) for each particular sale (note that this implies, as the reality, that the decision-maker at an organisation may change depending on the particular circumstances or service being purchased). Like the DMU, the model considers the roles of users and technical buyers but also introduces the coach (your prime information source – someone within the buying organisation who will help you learn more about the buying organisation) which equates with earlier comments about sponsors.

2 RED FLAGS/LEVERAGE FROM STRENGTH

This involves undertaking a careful analysis of the client situation and identifying areas where problems may occur, as well as your key areas of strength. These potential problems may arise from, for example, weaknesses in your offering, weak links in the relationship, buyers with whom you are unfamiliar or competitor activity. For example, a red flag may be that you have no contacts with the individuals in a particular department of the client organisation and a strength may be that you have worked with a very similar organisation for many years and therefore have no learning curve and possibly some 'best practice' knowledge of their particular problems.

3 RESPONSE MODES

This is where you must anticipate the client's reaction to your proposals and to the implied need to change in some way – the term 'reality-results discrepancy' is used. Response modes include growth (We need this service to help us grow), trouble (We need this service because we must act to avoid a crisis), even keel (There is no need for this service at present), or overconfident (Everything is OK and there is no issue for us at present so we do not need this service). The model offers strategies to deal with clients in different response modes.

4 WIN-RESULTS

This relates to the point made frequently in this book that in the professions we are concerned with long-term relationships (satisfied clients, repeat business, good referrals etc.). Therefore, we must not compromise that long-term relationship to achieve a short-term sale with which the client is not entirely satisfied. In all situations there must be a win for the buyer and a win for the seller.

5 IDEAL CUSTOMER PROFILE

Closely aligned to the marketing process, this aspect encourages you to think about your ideal clients so that you avoid trying to sell your services to inappropriate clients or to anticipate problems in your current client portfolio. It helps you sort out the worthwhile prospects from the no-hopers, thus increasing your sales effectiveness.

6 SALES FUNNEL

The feast-famine cycle is a common problem for the professions – one minute you have far too much work and the next you have nothing. In Chapter one the client relationship ladder was shown and it was mapped onto the marketing, selling and client development processes. The basic idea is that to maintain a constant and even stream of new business you need to ensure that you have clients at each stage of the cycle. This approach offers a good approach to keeping track of the various sales opportunities within your organisation and managing future sales forecasting.

This approach has a range of excellent training courses from the basic concepts of selling, through planning strategies for particular complex selling opportunities onto approaches for dealing with major accounts (LAMP-Large Account Management and Planning). Professionals I know who have been through the course valued the structure it bought to the analysis of a selling situation and the concepts they could use to discuss live sales situations, but found the process (a variety of different coloured forms) to be somewhat burdomsome.

RADAR™

Rick Page is founder of The Complex Sale Inc, which is well known for its range of sales training workshops. It is focused on selling solutions to multiple buyers in competitive evaluations (i.e. pitches and tenders) with an emphasis on competitive positioning, politics and power and team selling situations for winning new business. They have developed a specialist approach for professional service firms – in conjunction with a number of leading management consultancies to support their sales efforts – but we discuss here the general principles.

RADAR™ addresses the specific issues arising in team selling situations, provides 10 laws of team selling and explains the need for technique, talent, teamwork and technology. It offers an excellent individual development plan template.

The technique recognises the need for a good marketing strategy (see Chapter two) and there is much emphasis on understanding your 'arsenal of competitive advantage'. It explains how advantages must be linked to the personal agendas of the right people. He raises an interesting point that "you don't always need product or service superiority to win – but that you must have a greater understanding of the client's business than ever before". It suggests that the role of marketing and "product design" is to give a sales force as large an arsenal of advantages and benefits as possible.

The RADAR™ process (Reading Accounts and Deploying Appropriate Resources) offers six keys to winning a sales opportunity:

CHALLENGES	RADAR PROCESS
Value	**1** Link solutions to PAIN (or GAIN)
Resource allocation	**2** Qualify the PROSPECT
Competition	**3** Build competitive PREFERENCE
Strategy	**4** Determine the decision-making PROCESS
Politics	**5** Sell to POWER
Teamwork	**6** Communicate the strategic PLAN

There are useful strategies for linking solutions through urgency, differentiation, value and politics, awakening dormant pain and the 'so what?' test (see Features and benefits in Chapter six). A particularly powerful mechanism for separating strategic from tactical pain is the shark chart of the food chain of value. One observation is that pain does not come from the business problem itself but from the political embarrassment it causes, and there are suggestions for how to 'peel back the layers of pain'.

The process prompts you to put aside natural optimism to take an objective look at the chances of getting the work and stresses the need for asking tough questions early to disqualify rather than wasting resources pursuing a 'no hoper'.

Help in creating preference starts with a reminder of the psychological principal by Ries and Trout, that it is many times easier to help someone make up their mind in the first place than it is to change it. It advocates critical thinking into how your competitors will try to defeat you and counsels care in selecting the first point of entry (as you can't go higher easily). Initially building rapport leads to credibility, which leads to trust and enables you to influence the evaluation process. There are some good examples of tackling the thorny problem of a constantly delayed decision. Ideas around power draw on lots of nuggets from other gurus (e.g. Covey, Mintzberg, Handy, Levitt etc) and addresses issues around shadow or invisible power structures and the value of reciprocity, social interaction, charisma and integrity.

There is a good dynamic strategic plan model (information, vision and mission, goals, objectives, strategy, tactics, plan test, execution, results monitoring) and a reminder from 'Why CEOs fail' that often they are from a marketing/sales background and fail to seek or deal with bad news (e.g. through a curbside review).

Developing and communicating the sales strategy is a stage that is often omitted but there are excellent strategies for execution and much pragmatic advice. The strategies are broadly as follows:

GENERAL CATEGORY	SPECIFIC STRATEGY	COMMENTS
Pre-emptive	Demand creation rather than demand reaction	Winning the battle before it starts
	Ask for and seek an exclusive or sole source evaluation. Align yourself with a power partner. Walk away early	
Frontal strategies	Sell the product, proposal or company story	Only works when you have superiority
Flanking strategies	Change the pain, power, process, linking solutions or expanding the scope	Bringing your strengths against competitors' weakness
Fractional strategy	Partnering	Divide and conquer Appropriate for selling to Government
	Divisional	
	Penetrate and radiate	
Timing	Delay	
	Accelerate	

There is a good warning that the issues change in relative importance during a long sales cycle (screening, information and analysis, decision-making, acquisition and commodification stages) and the increasing interest in risk and pricing negotiations as the decision draws closer. To support the generic 'opportunity' strategies there are also ten strategies for focusing on the individuals involved in the decision-making process.

It touches on the use of C-Level (i.e. chief executive officer, chief financial officer etc) executive sponsorship as a passport to account management by focusing on issues of importance to them – strategic, political, financial and cultural and exploring the different distinctions between satisfiers and differentiators. It offers a useful set of eight goals for enterprise level strategy – penetrate, demonstrate, evaluate, radiate, collaborate, elevate, dominate and innoculate.

The approach has much of value to professional firms – although it lacks the rigour of an underlying process for opportunity or client management such as that in strategic selling described above. It is not an approach that I would recommend to a complete sales novice (they would gain more from a more basic introduction to complex sales) but for an experienced professional who is looking to improve their existing sales effectiveness it is ideal. The approach is invaluable to business developers who must manage complex sales to large organisations and to marketers who act as coaches to professional teams in tendering or who are faced with a major sale that has somehow become 'stuck'.

Behavioural science systems

This approach emerged from research into client relationship management. The basic premise is that clients have four distinct requirements and each needs a different approach:

RELIABILITY

Emphasis on a consistent approach to quality, there is a fundamental belief that excellence sells itself.

TRUST BUILDING

Important where services are commoditised (i.e. little perceived difference between them) so the emphasis is on strong personal relationships.

BENEFITS

Focus on the positive aspects of your firm's services.

SOLUTIONS

Appropriate when the client has unusual or complex problems and concentrates on the development of a partnership between client and provider.

It is interesting that many professionals adopt the reliability and trust building approach to selling, yet the benefits and solutions approaches often yield much greater sales success and client satisfaction. However, the different approaches have a part to play in different selling situations (e.g. with new or established clients).

Summary

This chapter highlights just a few of the many different models, methodogies and approaches that have been developed over the years to improve the effectiveness of selling. Many were not developed with the needs of a part-time salesperson who's main focus in life is in the production and delivering of professional services. Some of the approaches do not accommodate the need to develop an ongoing relationship that is so important to professional advisers. However, each model described here has something to offer the professions – either in terms of developing a better understanding of what the buyer is seeking, providing a pathway through the complexity of a long selling cycle or offering strategies to deal with common situations that professional advisers face. In my opinion there is no one overall approach that meets exactly the diverse needs of the professions in all the new and existing client situations they face. However, a professional who has received in-depth training in one approach will know where they are weak and will be better able to 'mix and match' concepts and strategies from other techniques more easily.

SIX
Selling skills

ROADMAP

This chapter moves away from overall structures, processes and frameworks and considers a wide range of different skills and activities that take place during the selling process. Readers will probably wish to review only those sections where they are unfamiliar with the concepts or where they have a particular need or question. The selling skills covered include: setting objectives, targeting, researching, cold calling, networking, conversational skills, following up, building trust, non-verbal communication, listening, questioning, writing, presenting, persuading, negotiating, handling objections, closing and direct approaches.

So far in this book, we have considered the processes going on in the minds of the buyers and we have looked at some frameworks that help professionals structure and plan their approach to selling. At each stage they must draw upon a blend of rather different skills. This chapter identifies and considers some of the core skill groups and activities that can be supported by training to improve sales performance. Many of the topics below are large enough to merit training courses in their own right. They are addressed only briefly here but readers are encouraged to seek further information on topics of interest by consulting the book list in Appendix two.

As many of the activities described involve a number of different skills, there is an element of repetition to aid those readers who are reading this book selectively in search of information on particular issues.

Setting objectives

Many professionals complain that they are no good at selling but when I ask them to substantiate their 'failures' they cannot tell me what they set out to achieve. It is a bit like deciding to do some law, or accountancy, or surveying without knowing why or for whom!

Get SMART!

If you want to know whether you are successful in marketing or selling you will need something against which to measure yourself. Therefore you need some objectives and they should be Specific, Measurable, Achievable, Realistic and Time specific (**SMART**).

If you are just starting out, your objectives should not be too ambitious. Set something with which you feel comfortable. You might also set objectives for both the process of and the results of selling. For example:

PROCESS

Set up a database of existing clients	Week 1
Set up a database of prospects	Week 2
Research needs of clients and prospects	Week 3
Contact 20 prospects by mail	Weeks 4-6
Telephone to arrange appointments	Weeks 5-7
Meet five prospects	Weeks 7-10

RESULTS

Meet with three new clients	By quarter 1
Submit three proposals to prospects	By quarter 2
Convert one prospect into a client	By quarter 3
Win type X work from existing client A	By quarter 3

If you are more experienced at selling, then set some goals that will move you forward. If you are currently winning around 25% of your competitive tenders, then set a new target for winning 50% by a specific date. If you are good at getting in the door, but not so good at being asked to present proposals, then set objectives at increasing your hit rate.

Once you have set some objectives you must ensure that the relevant information and monitoring systems exist (see Chapter nine on Firm-wide issues on selling) so that you can keep track of your progress and take action if your strategies and approaches are not generating the expected results.

If you are focusing your efforts on developing more business from an existing major client then the guidance provided in Chapter eight on Account management will be helpful.

Chapter two on Marketing provides more information about setting marketing and sales objectives – particularly at a firm-wide or departmental level as opposed to individuals.

Targeting

Trying to sell without a list of targets is rather like going out hunting and then shooting indiscriminately into the trees. You would be far more effective if you took some time in advance deciding what you wanted to shoot and learning more about the habits of your prey (sorry to the anti-hunting readers for my distasteful choice of analogy!).

How do you target your prospective clients? My view is that this is an important and integral part of the marketing planning process and should happen in advance of any selling activity. Therefore, you should ensure you have a solid marketing plan (see Chapter two).

Good targeting will result from a careful review of your existing client base to identify common themes and needs, a strategic positioning review to see what clients value most from your firm when considered against the competition, a sound segmentation strategy (e.g. what particular market sectors or niches) and some creativity. You may find that your firm or your department already has a detailed marketing plan and list of major clients and key targets and your role is simply to identify those for which you will take responsibility.

An alternative approach is suggested by Maister (see Chapter five) – Just think of those clients that you would most like to serve. Who are your dream clients? What clients would you be willing (almost!) to serve for free? This will provide you with an ambitious target list – but one that you will feel passionate about pursuing. You can analyse your ideas of a dream client or think more deeply about the existing clients that you have and value most to come up with a list of criteria that provides an 'ideal client profile'. This profile can then be used to seek suitable prospects and reject those where you do not wish to waste time.

However, if your firm does not possess an existing list then your first step is the use of a database (sometimes called a CRM – Client Relationship Management system) to capture, organise and classify information about your existing clients. Secondly, you should then analyse and grade (in terms of importance – you might also use the sales funnel concept to help here) your prospects and existing contacts (some of you will have to target referrers or intermediaries rather than the end user clients). Typically, a senior professional will have a client and contact list that can comprise several thousand clients and contacts. However, you will only be able to devote sufficient time to 'convert' a limited number of prospects into clients so you should have a short list of those targets you plan to focus on.

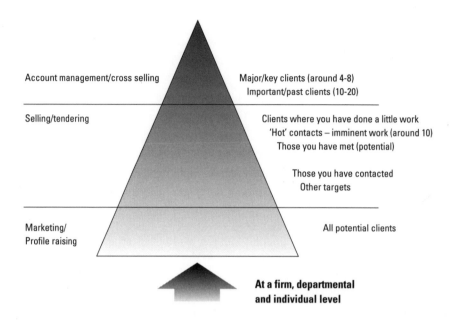

Account management/cross selling — Major/key clients (around 4-8)
Important/past clients (10-20)

Selling/tendering — Clients where you have done a little work
'Hot' contacts – imminent work (around 10)
Those you have met (potential)

Those you have contacted
Other targets

Marketing/
Profile raising — All potential clients

**At a firm, departmental
and individual level**

**FIGURE 18: MANAGING YOUR CLIENTS AND CONTACTS
AND DEVELOPING A TARGET LIST** (© KIM TASSO 2000)

You might also trawl around your firm to uncover additional contacts that are relevant. Make sure you co-ordinate your efforts with others in your firm who might also be targeting the same clients – the co-ordination of international clients and targets will increasingly become an issue as professional firms continue to consolidate across international boundaries (see Chapter nine on Firm-wide issues on selling).

If you are approaching a new market or area, then you will need to obtain information about the likely targets, for example, by obtaining a list of potential prospects. This might be through an external mailing list, an Internet or web based list or the subscription list to a magazine. You might do your own research to compile this list. These are marketing functions and you should seek the necessary support to undertake the process efficiently and effectively.

Then you should undertake detailed research (see below) to ensure you have as much information as possible about your prospects.

Researching

Gathering information about markets, clients, prospects and competitors is a vital stage in the marketing process (see Chapter two) but is also important in selling, both to prepare appropriate opening contacts or to address the needs of a client within the context of a competitive tender. Research is a vast subject in its own right, with many different disciplines and skills. Firms will differ in the amount of information they have about their market and existing clients – and whether it is in the form of accessible systems, stored in manual client files or in the heads of the senior partners. Firms will vary too in the research resources they have access to and can afford. Too often firms fail to involve junior members of staff in the research process where they can provide a cost-effective resource and increase their understanding of the firm's markets and clients.

Primary research

Primary or 'field' research is where you go direct to the clients intermediaries or potential clients, to obtain information. You might use a questionnaire to structure face-to-face or telephone research or you may have discussions amongst groups of clients and prospective clients (i.e. focus groups or client advisory panels). There are advantages and disadvantages of each method. Sometimes you will need to commission the services of a professional market researcher to assist you and there are market research consultancies who specialise in research in the professions. Where external researchers are used you will need to prepare a detailed brief of what you want to obtain and you will need to be sure that the researchers are experienced in dealing with the types of interviewees you propose, and in the nature of the professional relationship you have with those clients.

Typically, this sort of research is undertaken centrally within the firm or with the assistance of the marketing department. Some professional bodies (e.g. The Law Society) undertake primary research that can then be used by those in the professions, so always check to see what already exists before embarking on a primary research exercise.

Good practice in research will ensure that you define your objectives at the outset, have a clear brief in terms of who you want to reach and why, and what you will do with the research results obtained. Some firms undertake research purely to inform their own strategies, whilst others use some or all of the research material to generate publicity and to act as a platform for other marketing activities such as seminars and booklets. Care should be taken when the objectives of the research become confused – some firms request an interview on the basis of doing research and then attempt to sell their services – not very ethical behaviour.

Primary research focusing on in-depth interviews with existing key clients can achieve a number of objectives.. First, the results of these interviews can be used as the start and basis for developing an account management plan or a client relationship management process (see Chapter eight on Account management). It can form the start of a new dialogue with existing clients about how you can improve their satisfaction and perhaps help your cross-selling strategies. Secondly, the general findings and conclusions from these interviews can be used to inform your general marketing and sales strategies – helping you see the strengths and weaknesses and particular benefits in your approach that are valued by existing clients that can be communicated to prospective clients (see Marketing in Chapter two).

Appendix four contains an example questionnaire that may help you define and shape your primary research exercises.

Secondary research

Secondary or 'desk' research is where you use existing information that has been obtained for another purpose. There are a myriad of sources and the amount of information becoming available on the Internet adds to this. Some firms will have libraries, information officers, market research officers or knowledge managers who will have expertise in knowing where to look for different types of information. Smaller firms will find considerable assistance at local reference libraries (with directories such as Dunn & Bradstreet, Key British Enterprises and Kompass) or at local Chambers of Commerce, Training and Enterprise Councils (TECs) or Business Links. Many business and professional associations offer excellent printed and on-line research tools – the Institute of Directors is a good example. It is important to exhaust the secondary research sources before embarking upon primary research.

If you are researching a market, you will find assistance in a number of sources. Many markets will have trade, commercial or professional associations who have gathered much information about the market in question. There will be specialist research and information agencies where the information you seek is already held. On-line sources can be good too, although it may take some time to find exactly what you seek as the search engines often leave a lot to be desired.

Another valuable way to learn more about your clients, their competitors and markets and the business issues they face, is to read their industry journals. In addition to obtaining contact details, recent news coverage of your clients and prospects will provide you with valuable insights to shape your selling strategy or to identify new needs and issues that may be sales opportunities. Increasingly, commercial clients require their advisers to have a really indepth knowledge of their business and industry and regular reading of business, trade and technical press can support this.

If you are researching a mailing or cold calling list you will obviously need to obtain address, telephone and email details and the name of the person in the job function you wish to contact. Some sources may be old so you may consider using telemarketing services to update or 'clean' your list. It will be helpful too to gather as much background information as you can – turnover, number of employees, location of offices, overseas interests, nature of products and services sold, existing advisers, policies and procedures etc. Much of this information can be obtained from an organisation's website or you may wish to request copies of annual reports and brochures. It will make it much easier too if all the information that is collected is organised and kept in a methodical way, for example, in a marketing database or CRM (see Chapter nine).

Cold calling

Cold calling strikes fear into the hearts of most professional people – and so it should, for in some professions cold calling by telephone or in person is still forbidden. You must check your professional rules before embarking on a cold calling campaign. For example, it was only during the last year that The Law Society allowed cold calls to commercial organisations and it is still forbidden for solicitors practices to cold call members of the public. There may also be professional rules forbidding you to pay a third party for leads or appointments generated on your behalf. You should also be aware that any database of information you possess or develop, to support telemarketing campaigns will be subject to the Data Protection Act, which has severe financial and criminal penalties. There are also penalties for firms who do not check their databases against the Telephone, Fax or Mailing Preference Services and remove those individuals and organisations who have indicated that they do not wish to receive contact this way. If you are completely new to telemarketing and are planning a major campaign or investment in it, then you would be well advised to use the services of an experienced and professional telemarketing agency.

I would also advise professionals that they embark on some other method of initiating contact with their targets. For example, a direct mail programme to offer newsletters or invitations to seminars or events would be a good initial contact point. Then you will have a chance of meeting and talking to the targets in person rather than trying to establish contact, credibility and interest during a rather short telephone conversation.

However, if you decide to proceed with a telephone cold calling campaign your marketing programme (see Chapter two) should enable you to identify your targets and obtain a suitable list. Some preliminary research should be undertaken in advance to both:

a) clean the list (i.e. to ensure that it is up-to-date and accurate and shows the names of the key contacts) and

b) provide you with some background that will enable you to make a successful call.

Here are some things that will increase the chances of a successful cold call:

Advance preparation

Before making the call there are a number of preparatory things you should do:

RESEARCH

Find out as much as you can about the organisation and the individual you are contacting. It is important that you identify the correct decision-maker and are ready also to deal with any gatekeepers who may intercept your call.

SET OBJECTIVES

Be clear about what you want to achieve in the call. Avoid getting into a situation where you are forced to describe your services or firm in detail on the phone. Ideally, the call should be designed to get the recipient to agree to some low commitment action (e.g. read a letter you are about to send, attend a workshop, agree to an appointment etc.) as quickly as possible.

IDENTIFY A TOPIC OF INTEREST

Be as specific as you can about the nature of the call. If you have noticed in the media that the organisation is having difficulty (or success) then moulding what you have to say to be relevant to this is a good strategy. A general 'this is the range of services we offer' type of call is rarely likely to be successful. Your call should focus on a clear need. Your aim in the call is to promote some form of dialogue that either provides you with further information and/or enables you to agree some action.

REHEARSE WHAT YOU WILL SAY

Note down the key points you wish to cover when you make the call and rehearse a few times whilst anticipating the different sorts of responses you are likely to receive. The use of a script is not recommended as it can make professionals sound stilted and artificial. The more times you rehearse and the more alternative responses you work through, the more confident you will feel and sound.

MAKING THE CALL

Make sure you are in a comfortable and quiet environment where you can concentrate on the conversation and where you will not be distracted by noise or other matters. Ensure you have a pen and paper handy to note down any key points that arise and that you have a prompt list showing the key things you intend to cover.

INTRODUCTIONS

Introduce yourself and your firm clearly and confidently. A smile will be heard on the other end of the phone line. You should prepare a suitable presentation and practice saying it confidently before making a call. Make sure your voice sounds friendly, professional and authoritative.

VERIFY THE PERSON YOU ARE SPEAKING TO

Check that the person you are speaking to is the right person (e.g. 'Are you responsible for managing your organisation's professional services?'). It is polite to ask whether they can spare a few moments to speak or to ask for a time when you can call back.

GETTING PAST GATEKEEPERS

You may have to explain why you are calling to one or more gatekeepers whose role is to protect their superiors from cold calls. The strategy you adopt for this will depend on both your own style and that of the person who is doing the screening. Research or the use of intermediaries may enable you to bypass gatekeepers. You can develop a rapport with the gatekeepers and obtain information about the person you are trying to speak to that will increase your chances of success.

CHECK THE TIMING OF THE CALL

Think about the best time to call – early morning, mid morning, just before lunch, early evening etc. Once you have reached the decision-maker, confirm that they have a few minutes to talk. If they sound busy or harassed ask them what would be a better time to call (and make sure you call back at the agreed time).

GENERATE INTEREST

Use the AIDA (Attention Interest Desire Action – see page 35) model to structure your call. Like all selling, ensure that you address their needs and concerns rather than spending a lot of time talking about you or your firm. Again, make the topic as specific as possible and relate it to the person or organisation you are calling.

LISTEN

Like all sales situations, you should listen carefully to what is being said. On the phone you do not have the advantage of being able to see non-verbal communication (see page 123) so it is much more difficult to build trust and rapport. Take notes during the call if it helps you concentrate.

END THE CALL

Whether or not you achieve the objective of your call, you should make sure you retain control and signal the end of the call. Offer thanks for their time and confirm what follow-up action will be taken (this should be noted in your brought forward system or, better still, on the marketing database or contact management system you are using to organise all your sales information).

AFTER THE CALL

Make a note of the key things that emerged during the call (preferably in your marketing database which will also have an integrated brought forward/reminder system). Complete any immediate actions (e.g. write an email or letter confirming the call or send the information that was requested). Think whether the call went well or not and how you should modify your approach for future calls.

Networking

Many professionals ask for advice and guidance on improving their networking skills and effectiveness. A key issue is often the selection of appropriate events at which to network. The choice of appropriate environments in which to network would be a marketing function (see Chapter two). The networking skills you need are somewhat different depending on whether you are networking in an environment where you are the host and already know a large number of delegates (e.g. an in-house seminar) and where you are a guest at someone else's event.

You should be aware that networking is unlikely to generate immediate sales leads. By networking you can raise the profile of your firm, obtain market intelligence about competitors or your prospects and make contact with people who may assist your selling activities at a later date. You may even use networking to identify opportunities for other jobs and careers. Networking can be undertaken by both senior and junior people – helping them develop 'people skills' that will be valuable in all aspects of business, professional and social life. Networking is rarely effective if treated as a one-off activity or immediate results are expected. Networking is a vast subject in its own right – drawing on many interpersonal and selling skills. We can only take a relatively superficial look at this vast subject.

Preparation

Obtain a list of delegates before you attend so you can be familiar with the types of individuals (and their organisations) you are likely to meet. This can assist in the difficult area of name badge gazing. It is also a good idea to prepare to talk about a few topics likely to be of interest – ideally about the context of the event but also about current affairs. Some people will review the delegate list to identify who they are most keen to meet and then ask the organisers to help with identifying and introducing the chosen individuals. You might also invest some time undertaking research on the delegates before you attend – armed with such information will enable you to look informed and to ask pertinent questions. Some people even telephone those they know will be attending and indicate that they would like to meet them at the event.

Set objectives

Your specific aims should be dictated, in part, by a proper marketing analysis and marketing plan (see Chapter two). Typical aims might include:

MEETING NEW CONTACTS

- To find out some particular information?
- To establish rapport?
- To create the right impression of your firm?
- To gain commitment to some future action or meeting?
- To broaden your contacts within a particular organisation or industry?

MEETING ESTABLISHED CONTACTS

- To thank them for their past work?
- To determine what future work there might be?
- To introduce them to your colleagues or other clients?
- To build a friendship?
- To entertain them?
- To ask them to refer you?
- To learn more about what they think of you/your firm?

Arriving

You can achieve an advantage by timing your arrival at an event carefully. An early arrival means you will probably receive the undivided attention of a large number of the hosts. It means you will also find it easier to start conversations with other early arrivals. However, often the most senior people will not arrive until later in the event. Those at the end of the event are likely to be the experienced networkers or close friends of the host and therefore useful contacts, as they will typically have a wide circle of other contacts into which you can connect.

Making an approach

How you break into a group or start a conversation is a question that people frequently ask. With groups, you should watch to see how physically close they are to each other – those who are very close to each other are signalling that they do not want others to join their conversation. Watch also for the intensity of the conversation so you can speak when there is a natural lull in the conversation. Some people prefer a direct approach such as "Hello, may I join you?" whilst others will use gestures and smiles to listen to what others are saying. You can use various strategies such as "Excuse me and apologies for interrupting, but does anyone know where I might find Mr X or Ms Y?" or even "Excuse me but I would really welcome the opportunity to ask you about x". Sometimes you can ask the organisers or other people to break into a group or introduce you.

Introductions

Pronouncing your name and firm clearly (and with a smile) and providing conversation hooks are things that can be practised and rehearsed in a safe environment. Learning to introduce your colleagues (rather than yourself) provides the opportunity to offer much more information than when introducing yourself. The 'elevator' technique is sometimes useful (i.e. how would you describe your firm or value if you had 90 seconds with a chief executive in an elevator?).

First impressions

Try not to make quick initial impressions about whether someone at an event is worthy of your attention (see Perception in Chapter four). Over 70% of the meaning in any interaction is from non-verbal communication (i.e. appearance, gestures, body stance, tone and pitch of voice, eye contact etc.) so develop your understanding of this area. The way you feel (i.e. positive or negative, confident or nervous) will have a big impact on your non-verbal communication and the way others perceive you. You can use techniques (e.g. NLP – Neuro Linguistic Programming) to help you develop confidence. There is considerable evidence to show that first impressions are formed very quickly (just a few seconds) and that it is incredibly hard to change the first impression once established. Sometimes people who look uncomfortable and remain on the periphery are there because they dislike the networking scene as much as you do. Introducing yourself, showing an interest and helping them to network further can help them feel more at ease and indebted to you.

Hunt in a pack

Ideally, networking should be done in pairs or groups as 'lone' guests always feel and look a bit distant. Working together means you are unlikely to be left alone and that you can more easily join other groups of people than if you were alone. You can also use the introduction of your colleague as a way to move on to other people.

Show interest and ask questions

Most professionals feel inadequate at making small talk although they can rely on asking interested questions about other people's views, roles, organisations and industries to keep the flow of conversation going. Various non-verbal cues can be used to show interest. Open ended questions are good at getting conversations started and finding areas of common interest.

Memory

Many professionals worry that they will not remember names or points discussed at a networking event. Occasionally excusing yourself to write rapid notes on the back of business cards or in your personal organiser – or at least immediately after the event, will assist. There are various techniques that can be learned to help with memory improvement.

Low commitment follow-up

You will not always need to obtain a business card and asking for one without a clear reason is often met with suspicion (as is the unprompted offering of a card). Asking for a meeting or lunch appointment on the basis of a brief chat is unlikely to meet with success as it is too high a commitment. Prepare a number of low commitment follow-ups (e.g. 'I think I saw an article on that recently – I could send it to you' or 'My colleague would know about that, can I get him/her to give you a call?') that will provide a reason to obtain contact details and implicit permission to contact the person later. It is also a good idea to have a range of things that can be sent to people met in this way shortly after meeting – without necessarily requesting a meeting at that stage.

Ending conversations

Once you have spoken to someone for sufficiently long you need to be confident in how you end the conversation and move onto other people. There are various approaches. The direct and honest approach would be "Well, it has been really good to meet you and I will send you that information but now I must try and meet with some other colleagues here". Other methods might be to suggest that you approach other people and mingle together. Some people excuse themselves to visit the loo or get a drink – in the hope that others will have joined the conversation on their return and have thus released them. You might use the opportunity to introduce your colleagues or other contacts you know to the person.

Confidence and positive mental attitude

Neuro Linguistic Programming (NLP) involves understanding whether people's preferred mode of communication is visual, audio or kinesthetic and then matching their style. It uses visualisation techniques to help people regain positive feelings from good experiences to apply in new situations. There are other ways to encourage people to think positively before they attend a networking event and the positive mental state will be reflected within their subsequently more positive body language. In networking situations, people generally avoid those individuals who are giving off negative or uncomfortable vibes through their body language.

Long-term expectations

Networking can also be made much more comfortable if you remove the pressure of expecting to meet valuable contacts at events who will yield immediate results. Most effective networking takes place by putting other people together or providing information that has no short-term benefit to you or your firm. Networking should be seen as a way to widen the pool of contacts (the start of a pipeline) and as a starting point for the development of a long 'courtship'. A sustained effort to maintain contact (perhaps through a marketing programme) will build familiarity, trust and knowledge with a new contact.

Giver's gain

Networking is most effective when you develop a reputation for being someone who always has something to give – such as help in finding some information, ideas on other people who might help, useful introductions to possible clients etc. By helping those who you have met in a networking environment – with no immediate reward for yourself – you will build a bank of goodwill and favours which will hopefully be repaid at some point in the future. People will often remember those who have helped them and will watch for opportunities to repay such kindnesses.

Follow up

After a networking event, make sure you fulfil any actions you undertook – sending information, writing a quick email or making telephone calls. If you leave any actions for more than a week it may be difficult to pursue the opportunity. This is particularly important if you have been asked to get someone else in your firm to make contact. You should enter any information you have obtained into your marketing database or contacts system and you should grade new contacts on their importance (e.g. high, medium, low). You should also review how successful the event was in terms of your overall objectives and think how your experience can be applied to make future networking more effective.

Conversational skills

Some professionals may feel inadequate at making conversation in social or semi-social situations because they feel they cannot make 'small talk'. It is true that not everyone is a born raconteur who can keep an audience enraptured for hours but everyone can develop the confidence to make interesting conversation in any situation. There are various tips to assist:

Focus on the positive

Avoid talking about negative things (e.g. 'Wasn't the speaker dreadful?', 'Don't you think the food was cold?') as the negativity attaches itself to you. Identify the positive issues to discuss. Offer compliments (e.g. 'That is a very smart laptop case').

Feel good about yourself

In addition to feeling confident about yourself, you should also like yourself. This relates to the NLP ideas – if you feel positive about yourself and your ability to maintain conversations, you will communicate this through your non-verbal communication (NVC) and it will become a self-fulfilling prophecy.

Be sincere

The most important thing in all selling situations is to be sincere. If you are genuinely interested in a person you will find it easier to talk to them.

If you can fake sincerity you've got it made.
GROUCHO MARX

Don't interrupt

It is impolite to try to interrupt someone who is speaking. Even if what they are saying is dull, you must show interest and let them finish before attempting to ease the conversation in a different direction.

Use positive non-verbal communication

You can use NVC to show interest, to demonstrate enthusiasm and to express confidence and pleasure. People who gesture with their hands do so more when they are talking animatedly and enthusiastically.

Avoid talking excessively about yourself

Make sure you do not talk too much about yourself and your views, balance the information flow by encouraging the person to share their interests and ideas with you.

See opportunities to learn

If you see every interaction as an opportunity to learn something new, you will find that you ask questions that stimulate conversation. This way, every encounter has some value and you will find networking more rewarding.

Provide hooks

As you introduce yourself and start a conversation, provide lots of conversation hooks (e.g. your area, your firm, your line of business, your interests etc.) to help the other person pick up on topics of mutual interest.

Ask questions

Asking people about non-contentious issues such as their role, their organisation and their industry, or their views on current events usually promotes conversation. You might also ask them for their opinions on topical subjects.

Make people feel important

A key way to do this is to remember and use their name and, if you have met them before, recalling details that they have provided previously. Asking for people's views shows you value their opinion. Avoid scanning the room looking for other people while talking or listening as this is rude and indicates that you do not feel that the person you are speaking to is important or interesting.

Listen carefully

See the section on active listening.

'Seek first to understand' is one of the seven habits of highly effective people in the successful book by Stephen Covey. Showing interest, asking questions and listening carefully to people is one of the best ways to both develop your understanding of people and their organisations, and also in winning their trust and confidence.

Be interested rather than interesting

> *You will win more business in two months by becoming interested in other people than you can in two years by trying to get other people interested in you.*
>
> **DALE CARNEGIE**

Following up

Professionals often ask me how they follow-up after a chance meeting at a networking event or a meeting. This always surprises me as I would hope that either:

a) you had identified what you would like the ideal 'next action' to be **before** the meeting took place; or

b) had **agreed with the prospect** what follow-up action would be taken at the end of the encounter.

Without either of these it will be difficult to find a suitable follow-up action with which you would be comfortable.

Therefore, you should start planning your possible follow-up actions before you even meet your prospect. Ideally, if you have a marketing plan and have arranged an event as part of the marketing or sales programme (see Chapter two), you will have anticipated how you will follow up contacts afterwards. For example, you may have offered to send people a copy of some handout notes or to prepare a short paper on a topic that emerged during the course of the discussion. This part of marketing planning is concerned with campaign planning – so there are no 'one off' chance encounters, just a series of opportunities to interact with prospects over a period of time (Note: most sales frameworks – see Chapter five – will have a series of follow-up actions which gradually move closer towards a final sale).

If you attend a networking event, you should have in mind a number of potential low commitment follow-up ideas. Lunch or a meeting are high commitment ideas – people rarely wish to commit to a lunch or meeting on the basis of a short encounter. However, they are more willing to agree to read an article or brochure that you might be able to send if it relates to their interests or needs or, better still, if you are able to offer them a contact who may be able to help them in another area. Those people with a good knowledge of the brochures, materials, skills, client case studies and general information available across their firm will be much better placed to identify a suitable low commitment follow-up – which is where your internal communications programme comes into its own. Without some idea of a low commitment follow-up, it will be difficult to offer your business card to someone or to request one ('Why are you giving me your card?' or 'Why does he/she want my card?').

Good follow-up actions also rely on you having found a need that you can then meet. So, in effect, a meeting and follow-up is a microcosm of the entire selling process. It means that in the short space of time when you talk at a cocktail party, you have to identify even a trivial need in order to be able to provide a sound reason for progressing to the next stage.

Another important point to remember is how quickly after an event you should arrange contact. Some form of follow-up contact after a week or so does not look too aggressive. However, if you leave it too long you are in danger of the person forgetting who you are and what you talked about.

Building trust

The importance of trust in the client-professional relationship is generally acknowledged, so it's worth examining models that explore this issue in more detail. One model indicates that the dimensions of trust are: credibility, helpfulness, integrity, loyalty, competence, equity, honesty, safety, honoured pledges and previous experience. You should consider how you will meet all these criteria in each selling situation.

Building trust takes time and it is supported if you have a good understanding of the personality and needs of the individual and their existing perceptions. Regular, planned contact over a period of time (see earlier information on the selling cycle) will be helpful.

Non-verbal communication

Non-verbal communication (NVC) – or body language as it is commonly known – is a much maligned subject. Although most people will be aware of it – some may even call it commonsense – a sensitivity to the non-verbal messages being given by buyers, and care in controlling your own body language, can provide a huge support to successful selling.

This is a huge subject and I can only provide a very brief introduction. However, you must be aware that body language is heavily dependent on context (e.g. a cold room will alter NVC significantly), culture (e.g. see below on personal space) and gender (e.g. research shows that women are more sensitive to and better able to read NVC than men).

Voice

The pitch and pace of voice – and indeed accents – play a huge role in perception. Typically, people who speak fast are considered more intelligent and a lower voice is regarded as having more authority than a high pitched voice. The loudness of your voice is often taken as an indicator of your level of confidence and authority. Women may need help in modifying their voice if they wish to receive the same level of respect as their male colleagues.

Eye contact

Maintaining the right amount and type of eye contact is vital in establishing trust and rapport. Looking 'shifty' results when eye contact is not maintained appropriately. Too much eye contact can be threatening and sometimes an indicator of deception. When addressing a group of people, it is important to 'lighthouse' by repeatedly scanning all the faces – to avoid people feeling left out. Eye contact is often used to direct conversations – giving cues to encourage people to speak and contribute or requesting an opportunity to speak. A real smile will be reflected in people's eyes and a false smile is easily detected.

Personal space

Imagine around each person there is a bubble of space into which others should not enter. You know how uncomfortable you feel when someone else is in your space (think of a crowded tube train). The amount of space you require is culturally determined and will be different depending on your country of origin (e.g. North Americans need a large space whereas those from the Middle East require a small space) and whether you are from an urban or rural background. The space issue is particularly important in social and networking conversations – ideally, you should tolerate discomfort in your body space if it makes the other person feel more at ease. Sometimes we feel uncomfortable about some people without realising why, this can be due to the fact that they speak to you too closely or too far away – i.e. in a different body space to that which you prefer.

Open and closed stance

If a person adopts a very 'tight' or closed (e.g. arms and legs folded against the body) stance – using as little space as possible – it indicates a lack of confidence as opposed to someone who uses a large space by extending their arms and legs into the surrounding space. If you appear 'closed' you will deter people from interacting with you. The way you stand or sit – and the amount of body space you take up – will have an impact on how confident you appear.

Barriers

Much as a desk presents a barrier between those on opposite sides, there are other personal barriers to watch for. Arms folded across the chest is a common example (although check it is not because the person is cold) and a modified version would be the cuff pull. Crossed legs can be perceived as barriers too. Crossed arms and legs are also a form of auto-contact suggesting discomfort or a lack of confidence.

Orientation

Most meetings take place around a table. Generally, if someone is sitting back they are disengaged or lacking interest in the subject matter being discussed. Suddenly sitting forward, as you would when you started to speak, indicates an increase in interest. Some people watch for movements forward as buying signals.

When meeting people in networking situations, there are differences between the way men and women approach others – either directly in front or from the side.

Displacement

When nervous or irritated, some people will exhibit displacement activities such as tapping fingers or pens, shuffling papers or jiggling feet. This is a sign that you have lost their attention. Fiddling with the hair (preening) is another sign of nervousness often associated with courtship behaviour (and therefore to be avoided at all costs in professional selling situations!). Avoid fidgeting.

Superiority

Power plays often involve achieving a height advantage e.g. asking someone to sit in a lower chair than your own or rising on to the tips of your toes when standing (a common habit of many barristers). The classic legal gesture of 'steepling' (it forces others to look at your eyes so you regain eye contact) is to be avoided and so are the hands clasped behind the head. Women may have a disadvantage in networking situations as they are usually shorter than their male colleagues.

Power lifts

Actions that draw others' attention to your eye level (e.g. raising a finger, spectacles or a pen) are a way to attract their attention.

Deception

There is scientific evidence indicating that those telling lies will reduce the amount of hand gesturing, may reduce or increase eye contact and will increase the amount of contact with their mouth and face areas.

Mirroring

When people copy or mirror each others' stance, gestures and actions (e.g. all picking up a glass at the same time) it is a sign that they enjoy a level of rapport. You can test the extent to which someone has rapport with you by making some gesture or changing your stance and see if they subconsciously follow suit.

Touch

Although many social rules (and legal constraints) surround touch it remains a powerful way to 'anchor' positive feelings. The handshake is the formal social ritual defining the only touching permissible in western business situations and there are many nuances here (e.g. dominant hand on top, length and firmness of grip giving positive or negative impressions, additional use of the other arm around shoulders indicating greater closeness etc.). Research has shown that even a light and unconscious touch – such as when handing someone some papers – will lead to the 'toucher' being perceived more favourably.

Listening

One of the maxims of effective selling is to spend at least 50% of your time (but preferably more) listening rather than speaking. A good reminder of this is that you have two ears and only one mouth! Yet active listening is an acquired skill and takes practice. Most professionals think they are good at listening – however, most professionals are good at hearing key things and this is quite different to active listening.

The human brain is incredibly powerful. If you have developed a hypothesis or view about someone or something then your brain will tend to filter out and not register any information that does not 'fit' your existing map of beliefs and heed only those inputs that support your beliefs. This is why initial perceptions and prejudices are so dangerous – your brain will work to reinforce and support your sometimes incorrect assessments. This means that you have to make a conscious effort to listen to and evaluate all the information that is provided when talking to people.

If you fail to listen carefully and attentively to prospects and clients then you may miss vital clues and you may make inappropriate assumptions. A key element of selling is asking appropriate questions at the appropriate time – it then follows that it is important to listen carefully to the response. By listening carefully, you will gather information about both the business and the personal needs of the person you are talking to. Careful listening will avoid you making mistakes and offering solutions and suggestions at the wrong time.

The following guidelines may assist:

ADOPT AN OPEN STANCE

Check the material on non-verbal communication above. An open stance means that you are relaxed and not making any barriers with your arms or legs or items of furniture. You should take a reasonable amount of body space to show confidence.

SHOW INTEREST

Sitting slightly forward and inclining your head to the side is an 'interested' position. Avoid having things that can distract you – like unrelated papers on your desk, a screen within your view or a window through which you can see people moving about.

MAINTAIN EYE CONTACT

Without staring into the person's eyes, you should focus on their face. In business situations you should be concentrating on a small triangle made of the person's eyes and nose. Looking towards the door, above their head, at your watch or anything else indicates a lack of interest. Eye contact is an important way to signal that either you wish to talk or that you expect the other person to speak.

SUMMARISE OR REPEAT KEY POINTS

To balance the flow of communication, occasionally summarise, paraphrase or repeat the key points to help maintain your concentration and also to show the person that you are listening to and absorbing their words. This will also check you have understood properly and provides the other person with an opportunity to correct any misunderstanding.

PROVIDE CONTINUATION PROMPTS

There are a number of things you can do and say which do not stop the other person speaking but encourage them to keep talking – you can smile, nod slightly and say things like 'I see', 'Ahem' and 'Go on'. If you ask a question, make sure you remain quiet while the person gathers their thoughts – too often people ask a question, are discomforted by the silence and then rush in before the other person has a chance to answer.

ELIMINATE DISTRACTIONS

If noise is preventing you from concentrating (e.g. traffic noise through an open window, a loud meeting in the next room etc.) then do what you can to reduce the noise so that you are not distracted.

ASK INTELLIGENT QUESTIONS

To clarify points you find difficult to understand, to obtain further elaboration or to prompt the person to speak again you should ask questions (see questioning below). It has been shown that your ability to listen attentively is reduced when you lack a piece of information, are confused about something or start thinking through possible answers in your mind. The nature and use of questions is a fundamental part of the SPIN® sales framework which is described in Chapter five.

TAKE NOTES

Check it is OK to take notes and make sure that note taking does not reduce your ability to maintain the required level of eye contact. As well as providing a record of the key points being made, taking notes shows that you consider what the person is saying to be important. By taking notes you are increasing the 'processing' that your brain is doing and this will increase your ability to retain the salient points.

AVOID PRECONCEPTIONS

Do not let your first impressions or initial views override your ability to accept what the person is saying that may contradict your views (see Perception in Chapter four). It is known that if you have preconceptions about an individual or what they are likely to say, then your mind will filter out only those things the person says that will confirm your initial view. Selective perception should be resisted in selling situations – keep an open mind.

MAKE SURE YOU CAN HEAR

If the person is speaking quietly or you are having to strain to hear, you will not be able to concentrate for very long. Your attention will drift and the speaker will cease to talk. So make sure you can hear easily.

USE YOUR EYES

Your eyes can signal attention, they can encourage a person to continue speaking, they can demonstrate empathy and they can give reassurance.

THINK ABOUT GOOD LISTENERS

Think about how those people who you consider to be good listeners act – what do they do? How do they maintain and show interest? What makes people open up to them?

DO NOT 'SWITCH OFF'

If you feel you are losing your concentration, do something to help you regain it. This may involve asking a question, taking a break or offering a view on something that has been said. When you switch off, your eyes will glaze over and the person who is speaking will detect your lack of interest and stop speaking.

Questioning

Many of the selling frameworks considered in Chapter five place great emphasis on being able to ask the right questions and listen carefully to the responses and then respond in an appropriate way. However, when someone is uncomfortable with this questioning it can feel artificial and uncomfortable for both the buyer and the seller.

Most professionals will have acquired some questioning skills as part of their professional training – particularly litigators and barristers. But the style and nature of questioning in professional selling situations is very different to that of a professional trying to obtain the relevant facts and information for their functional role.

Some sales books encourage you to ask open ended questions during the exploratory phase of a selling situation and closed questions when you are trying to obtain some commitment. However, you should be wary of such hard and fast rules.

Open ended questions

Rudyard Kipling's famous poem mentions the importance of 'Who, Why, What, Where, When and How' and these are the main ways to pose open ended questions. An open ended question cannot be answered with a short 'Yes' or 'No' answer and will therefore encourage someone to speak further and provide information.

These questions are best used at the preliminary stage of a sales encounter as they encourage the buyer to reveal their interests and needs and to provide the seller with clues about how to proceed. The SPIN® model (see Chapter five on Selling frameworks) uses this questioning technique heavily.

Closed questions

These are questions that are usually answered with a 'Yes' or 'No'. They can be used to confirm key facts (e.g. 'Are you responsible for maintaining the panel of external advisers?' or 'Does your organisation have a formal policy regarding this matter?') or they can be used to test or gain commitment (e.g. 'Are you happy for me to continue?' or 'Are you comfortable with the pricing information I have given?'). Often, a closed question will reveal a reluctance or misunderstanding and provide an opportunity for you to correct the situation. Sometimes, closed questions will elicit an objection (see below).

Example questionnaires and questions to use when exploring a client's attitude to existing services are provided in Appendix four.

Writing skills

Whether it is a short letter of introduction, a longer email summarising the key points from a meeting, a detailed proposal or a response to a formal tender, writing is an important skill to aid selling. There are other writing skills needed for marketing – such as the style adopted in preparing media statements (which requires journalistic or public relations training) and in writing copy for advertisements, brochures or direct mail letters. These skills are very different to those most professionals use for their formal reports. The different types of writing involve very different styles and accepted practices so the only general training that is appropriate is in terms of grammar and report writing.

At the initial stages of selling there are models and techniques that can be adapted from direct marketing to assist. A good example is AIDA.

Attention Interest Desire Action (AIDA)

This provides a formula for writing letters that generate results. Too often professionals will write letters that are dull and heavy with text, contain too much information about the writer (rather than the reader) and which fail to interest the reader. An interest grabbing title (e.g. 'Tax savings bonanza for those who act quickly') or a question (e.g. 'Ready for the new legislation on paternity leave?') will obtain immediate attention. Many letters also say that the writer will call the reader after a few days whereas ideally the letter should prompt some low commitment action from the reader. Wherever possible, you should make it easy for the reader to respond by, for example, including a fax proforma, a reply paid envelope or an email/ web address.

A key issue is the adoption of the readers' point of view. Often, professionals write letters, documents and reports focusing on what they want to say rather than what the reader wants to know. The frequent use of 'We', the inclusion of much boilerplate material about the firm and the focus on features (e.g. 'We have 20 experts in X', 'We have offices in Y' etc.) rather than benefits are indicators that the writer has not properly adopted the readers' point of view (see below on Persuading for more information about features and benefits).

Providing a positive tone is also important, consider the difference between 'If we were to be appointed we would' to 'We will'. Active verbs and short sentences will convey confidence and provide reassurance.

Most professionals wish to demonstrate their knowledge by writing detailed explanations and including technical references. However, nearly all clients indicate their preference for short and relevant written material without any jargon! In an effort to be comprehensive, much written material is too long and verbose – always check that everything included is relevant to the reader (try the 'So what?' test and 'If in doubt, leave it out'!).

The critical issue with any form of writing is to ensure that you have a full and detailed understanding of the person you are writing to or for, tailor any information to their specific situation or needs and ensure that their interests and point of view is paramount.

Presentation skills

Most professionals are comfortable in a one-to-one meeting yet show concern at the prospect of making a formal or informal presentation to a small group. Ask them to present to a large audience and many go into a panic! There are many different issues surrounding effective presentations concerned with core skills, preparation, practice and confidence.

Professionals need to be trained in how to design and structure a presentation and then need guidance in how to prepare and present. Effective presentation is another huge topic in its own right – drawing on a variety of analytical, personal, selling and communication skills.

Where professionals are used to presenting as part of their day-to-day work (e.g. a barrister or expert witness in Court) it is important that they understand that the skills and style adopted may be very different if presenting at a promotional seminar, an external conference or at a sales meeting.

One of the most common mistakes is to try and present too much information. Regardless of how much information you have gathered as part of the research process or how much expertise you possess, you should identify the three to six key points you wish to convey and structure your presentation around these key points. If in doubt, leave it out! Repeating and reinforcing messages is important and the old adage 'Tell them what you are going to tell them, tell them and then tell them what you have told them' is useful to structure presentations. The other concept of 'KISS – Keep it Simple Stupid' is also relevant. A good test of a presentation's effectiveness is to ask a) what are we hoping to achieve with this presentation? and b) how will the audience feel at the end of the presentation?

A presentation is usually a one-way flow of information – from the presenter to the audience. However, in most sales situations your aim is to promote and sustain dialogue with the client. So you should avoid lengthy presentations where the 'audience' is forced to listen passively. Although it is more difficult to plan and control, your presentations should be interactive and promote questions and discussion.

Presentations should entertain as well as inform. You must convey some core information but you should also ensure that the listeners enjoy the experience. If you make a particularly powerful or humourous presentation you are more likely to be remembered than those who gave a more lack lustre performance. You can differentiate your firm significantly by your presentation performance.

You should acknowledge too that even with a large investment in training, some people are simply not comfortable and do not convey themselves well when presenting. Rather than force people to do things which they strongly object to (and have them perform badly and create a bad impression) it is best to choose those people who are more comfortable presenting.

There is a huge need for practice in presentations. The best presenters are often those who have a lot of experience in presenting and therefore are more confident. This can be easily and cheaply achieved by encouraging professionals from an early stage in their career by, for example, providing opportunities for them to present formally on a regular basis to internal audiences at departmental and other meetings.

Typically, presentation skills training would cover the following topics:

- Considering the target audience.
- Developing the title, theme and main content.
- Structuring the material.
- Preparing and using audio visuals (there may be a separate training session on using PowerPoint or other presentation software and hardware).
- Non-verbal communication.
- Introductions and conclusions.
- Addressing the audience.
- Projection, pitch and pace.
- Presenting the case (making ideas understandable, attractive and convincing).
- Relaxation and dealing with stress .
- Rehearsing.
- Handling questions.

Those attending presentation training are likely to be asked to prepare a short presentation in advance of the course. Not only does this force them to prepare in advance and think about the areas of difficulty they want to address, it is more likely to provide the trainer with a true reflection of the person's presentational style and ability.

Be careful to select a trainer who will build the confidence of the trainees rather than a trainer who destroys their self-confidence and creates a fear of public speaking that will haunt them forever.

Rehearsals are essential and videoing performance can help them identify weaknesses (and demonstrate improvement) in private. Often, individuals who are highly effective at presenting on their own do not perform so well when they are presenting as part of a team – which involves a slightly different approach and style. Rehearsing will prove useful here too.

The type of presentation skills needed in selling situations will be different depending on whether you are meeting the people for the first time (e.g. in cold calling or competitive tendering situations – see Chapter seven) or to people with whom you have a long standing relationship (see Chapter eight on Account development).

Persuading – features and benefits

There is much to persuasion as it is a complex communication process with many variables and interaction. A key to persuasion is empathy and seeing the buyers' point of view (see Chapter four).

There is considerable research around how to persuade effectively. For example, a two sided presentation is more effective with educated people (who are trained to resist a one sided argument) and a one sided presentation is more effective with less educated people. If you are presenting information from a variety of sources then the primacy effect will be observed (people tend to believe the first argument put forward rather than the most recent).

If you want to change someone's mind then you must have a really good understanding of how his or her mind is made up to begin with – the earlier information on empathy and research is relevant here. Be aware also that the effect of convincing others usually results in you convincing yourself – a useful thing to remember if you ask one of the contacts at your client or prospect organisation to persuade their colleagues of the value and merits of your proposals. You should also acknowledge that trying to persuade someone at the wrong stage of the decision-making process or buying cycle will result in discomfort and distrust and possibly an inelegant end to your sales efforts.

One of the most useful techniques in this area is the translation of features into advantages and benefits. The concept is appropriate for both written materials and for face-to-face communications. The best way to explain is through examples:

Features

- 'We have 40 offices throughout the world.'
- 'We have 25 experts in the specialist area of X.'
- 'We have a fully functional website.'
- 'We have acted for many clients in this sector.'

Features are very inward looking (notice how they usually start with the self important 'We') and concentrate on dislocated aspects of the service being offered without reference to their relevance to the recipient. In product selling it is equivalent to saying 'The car has four wheels', 'The car has side impact bars' etc. The natural reaction of the recipient is to say 'So what?' – and this is a good test to apply to any statements you make in any sales material or situation as it forces you to undertake the translation process.

So we translate features from their supplier focus into advantages and benefits with a buyer focus and in the process ensure that the relevance and usefulness of the features are made specific to the needs of the buyer.

Advantages

- 'We always have a professional close by.'
- 'Our in-depth knowledge of the subject.'
- 'Information is available 24 hours a day.'

Benefits

- 'This saves you time when seeking advice and reassures you that the professionals have the relevant local knowledge to find you the best offices.'
- 'This saves you time because the experts can formulate the correct response more quickly, plus you have the benefit of their best practice knowledge so you will be more confident that there will be no mistakes.'
- 'For standard queries, you or any of your staff can consult the private area of the website which means you can save a significant amount of money for simple enquiries.'

You will notice how the benefits statements nearly always address 'you' the client as opposed to 'we' the provider or seller.

For each client and selling situation there will be a different package of benefits. Developing a unique package of benefits (or unique selling proposition – USP) is important in differentiating your solution from those of your competitors. This topic is dealt with further in Chapter seven on Competitive tendering in 'What selling strategy to adopt?'.

FEATURES	ADVANTAGES	BENEFITS
We have worked for over 100 clients in...	• Lots of experience • Knowledge of best practice • Shorter learning curve • Less chance of errors	• You get a quicker or cheaper service • You get policy input or ideas • You feel secure
We are one of the largest firms in...	• Wide range of skills • Lots of resources • Economies of scale	• Easier/more convenient for you to have a 'one stop shop' • Always someone available for you • Your work gets done faster

FIGURE 19: THE 'SO WHAT?' TEST

Negotiating

Negotiation is a topic which causes much confusion in selling situations. Negotiation is 'conference and bargaining for mutual agreement'. In selling, the behaviours of seller and buyer are often totally different: persuader and persuadee. In negotiation, both parties use the same set of skills and behaviours because both have the same commitment to reach a workable agreement.

Some professionals receive a huge amount of training in negotiating as part of their professional role but seem unable to transfer these skills to selling situations. The area causing most concern is discussion about money and fees – which professionals nearly always resist.

In any negotiation there are only four outcomes:

1 Lose-Lose

2 Lose-Win

3 Win-Lose

4 Win-Win.

Where a professional adviser is looking to start and develop a long-term relationship with a client the only desirable outcome is 'win-win'. This means that both the client and the provider must be satisfied with the agreement reached. A client will not be happy if they feel they have had to compromise on some aspect of the standard of service or if the fees are too high. The provider will not be entirely happy unless they are able to advise the client on the particular issue where they have expertise or if the agreed fee does not reflect the input or generate sufficient profits. Therefore, negotiation must focus on ensuring that both parties come away from the discussions feeling they have 'won'. Some of the sales frameworks (see Chapter five) devote much time to achieving a successful win-win outcome.

Yet win-win requires more than a successful outcome to the agreement of the services provided. Individuals must feel they have 'won' on a personal level too. For example, a happy client is one who not only secures the best deal for the relevant legal or property advice, but who also feels that their choice places them in a favourable political position with the Board. A happy professional service provider is one who reaches a good deal with the buyer of his or her accountancy or consultancy services, and does so in a time frame that maximises their fee position at the right time of the bonus or promotion cycle.

Like other aspects of selling, negotiation is best approached with some structure and the following offers a possible methodology:

- Research.
- Prepare.
- Set objectives.
- Identify alternative course of action if negotiation fails.
- Prioritise the negotiable elements.
- Set your limits.
- Calculate the cost of concessions.
- Plan.
- Identify areas of mutual agreement and common aims.
- Assess the long-term relationship.
- Prepare to deal with issues in any order.
- Persuade (create instability and then move towards your view).
- Prepare questions.
- Analyse power.

Handling objections

In the section on questions I mentioned that objections may be revealed as a result of a 'test of commitment' question. Later on we can see that objections are sometimes raised when you are trying to 'close' a deal or negotiation.

Most people fear objections, seeing them as a barrier to the successful conclusion of a meeting or sale. They attach an undue importance to the objections – fearing that ultimate success or failure will depend on how they are handled. Some professionals may interpret objections as a more palatable way to say "No thanks". However, objections should be seen as opportunities. Sometimes they reveal a misunderstanding (which you can then correct) or are a route to providing additional information.

Sometimes prospects who have already made up their mind to proceed may raise objections either to confirm that their understanding is correct or to rehearse how they will sell the decision onto others in their organisation. In this case they are providing you with valuable insights into how the solution needs to be sold to others in the decision-making cycle.

There are a number of different strategies for dealing with objections, depending on the nature of the objection. For example, apart from a real objection ('I don't have any money') there may be false objections ('You don't have an office in Manchester' when really the location is immaterial) or hidden objections ('You don't have an on-line billing system' but really the client is uncomfortable with the senior partner) or frivolous objections ('It's going to cost a fortune!').

The strategies are:

- Listen carefully and do not interrupt.
- Pause and think before speaking – do not rush to offer defensive excuses.
- Clarify – Confirm your understanding of the issue and its importance on the sale.
- Classify – Is it a real, hidden or false objection? You may need to ask further questions to determine the nature of the objection. You may find that questioning and responding to false objections enables you to find the hidden objection.
- Counter, answer or confirm – adopt one of the following approaches:
  - Acknowledge (e.g. smile or nod your head to acknowledge a frivolous objection).
  - Re-phrase to ensure you understand the issue (e.g. 'So, if I understand properly your only remaining concern is about...'). This enables you to obtain more time to think and also more information about the specific nature of their concerns.
  - Agree (e.g. 'Yes, we are expensive but then this issue is critically important to your organisation and you will want the reassurance of a team that has dealt with this sort of transaction many times before').

- Straight denial (e.g. 'No, appointing us to assist with XYZ would not impact project C – I haven't explained myself properly...').

- Counter (e.g. 'Well, I would agree with you but if you are really concerned about X then we must see Y as secondary').

- Confirm – Check you have responded adequately. At this stage you may attempt a trial close (see below).

Other techniques include asking the client how they would deal with the problem 'So what do I need to tell you to reassure you on this point?' or 'How do you think we can overcome this issue?'. Another approach might be to test how important it is: 'Looking at the project overall, how critical is this particular issue'. This may not overcome the objection but at least it will enable the negotiation or sale to proceed.

A useful exercise for professional advisers is to list out all the general and specific objections that they hear most frequently and then get them to discuss possible responses with their peers and more experienced colleagues so that they exchange ideas and strategies. Asking your colleagues how they deal with a common objection such as 'But your firm is so much smaller than our current advisers' or 'We like to have only five firms on our approved panel'. Here is a selection of common objections provided by professionals at a recent training course – see if you can develop some ways to respond to and overcome the problems:

- 'You are too expensive.'

- 'I do not want to upset my current advisers.'

- 'It would be too difficult to transfer our work to you.'

- 'I do not really want to change advisers at this point in time.'

- 'But my current advisers are OK at present – I am not unhappy with them.'

- 'You are not on our panel of approved suppliers.'

- 'We do not perceive your firm as having expertise in this area.'

- 'I would be concerned to change advisers at this crucial point in time.'

- 'I have no need to change at present.'
- 'You only have one assistant with experience in this area.'
- 'Decisions about professional advisers must be referred to the purchasing department.'
- 'Our Board prefers to work with the larger/smaller firms.'

Closing

Closing is really about getting some form of commitment from the client. At some point in the sales process, you will have to ask for the business. This is often easier to do if you ask the relevant questions as you progress through a sale, rather than waiting until the end.

If you have followed one of the sales frameworks (see Chapter five) the opportunity should arise naturally, or you may find that the need to specifically request whether the business has been won has been averted as you simply progress towards a fee paying client relationship situation. With a structured sales approach each stage brings you closer to a natural conclusion – you will have learned at an early stage if you are unlikely to be successful and if you have remained in negotiations, which are focused on the clients needs, then you should end up where it is obvious that you will be awarded the work.

Some professionals get confused about closing – thinking of situations where they have known and been in contact with a potential client for a long time, without ever getting any business. This is not a closing problem but more likely due to the fact that they have not followed a sales strategy where a need is identified and a solution proposed. If this is the case then you should refer to the sales processes described in Chapter five.

Whatever the situation, this is the part of the sale that most professionals dread for it involves the possibility of rejection and failure (see Chapter three – Why is selling different for professionals?). Many professional people lack confidence in asking for the business. However, many clients comment that professionals do not win more business simply because they fail to ask for that business!

Non-verbal communication can be helpful in assisting you to identify buying signals which indicate that the client has made a decision and that you should quickly agree a way forward.

In classical sales training, you were offered a series of closing techniques which could be useful in professional situations if you wished to avoid asking the direct question 'Will we get the business?':

- **Client close**: 'So where do we go from here?', 'How would you like to proceed?'

- **Assumptive close**: 'When should we start?', 'When can you give us access to the information?'

- **Conditional close**: 'So, if we can reassure you about...', or 'So if the fees can be structured differently, you are happy to proceed?'

- **Directive close**: 'We will start reviewing the files immediately', 'I will let you have a revised timetable tomorrow'

- **Immediate gain close**: 'If we start today, we can...', 'By initiating action this month, you will...'

- **Summary close**: 'So, you will send us the relevant papers, we will start by speaking to X and then...'

Direct approaches

Increasingly, in the current market, firms are rejecting general forms of awareness raising marketing and indirect approaches to selling through networking and direct mail campaigns. They have developed such sophisticated marketing plans and sales strategies that they have identified a handful of organisations that they wish to do business with. They therefore need an approach that is much quicker than in the past – and much more direct.

What is interesting is that when you ask buyers how best new suppliers can make their offerings known to them they will tell you a direct approach. However, to do this effectively you must do a significant amount of research to uncover a need and make it very clear how you can meet this need (and in a way that their current advisers may not be able to do).

In effect, what you are doing is going through a very similar process to a competitive tendering process (the next chapter provides you with a methodology for doing this) but without the competition and submitting proposals on an unsolicited basis.

Nearly every research study shows – whether in the property, legal or financial sectors – that a carefully researched and well presented proposal document addressing a very real need for that client in a thoughtful or innovative way, will secure a meeting.

When we consider the decision-making process (see Chapter four) we can see that competitive tendering is at the later stage of evaluation of alternatives (where the client has already defined the problem, identified possible solutions and is asking you to present your case against their criteria and your competitors) whereas submitting an unsolicited 'tender' gets in at the earliest opportunity (perhaps before the client even recognises they have a need) and gives you much greater control over the decision process – and, if you are lucky, without the client considering alternative suppliers.

SEVEN
Competitive tendering

ROADMAP

This chapter takes professionals who are inexperienced at competitive tendering through the entire tendering process. As such it is most relevant to those who have to compete for work from commercial clients, although some private client firms may need to submit tenders for block allocations of work. After some preliminary consideration of the issues involved in tendering, the chapter takes you through a comprehensive 12 step framework which is designed to help professionals consider every element of the sales process within a competitive tendering situation. As such, the 12 steps draw on a wide range of selling concepts that are covered elsewhere in this book.

Introduction

A few years ago it was relatively rare – outside sectors such as construction or Government – for professional firms to be asked to submit tenders to clients in order to bid for work. However, nowadays it is quite common for even small firms seeking a small amount of advice to request competitive quotes. Similarly, it is quite common for clients to request their regular advisers to pitch – competitively – for ongoing work. Competitive tenders – like the clients who issue them – come in all shapes and sizes. Sometimes you are simply asked for a price and sometimes for a written document or a presentation. Sometimes the RFP (Request For Proposal) asks you to complete a long and detailed questionnaire – offering, apparently, little scope to differentiate your firm. Some firms use external consultants or have in-house teams to provide a high level of expertise when bidding.

Sometimes there is no formal tendering process but the client asks you to present some written proposals following an informal meeting. Sometimes, as we discussed in the previous section on direct approaches (see page 144) you may decide to prepare and submit unsolicited proposals on a particular issue although the client already has existing advisers in the same or a related area.

It is not appropriate to have a standard document or presentation for tendering as you will maximise your chances of success if each response is tailored to the particular client, their needs and the situation. This means that your success in tendering will be improved significantly if your firm has the relevant systems (such as on-line and regularly updated CVs and client case studies or computerised estimating systems – see Chapter nine on Firm-wide selling issues). This means that the professional responsible for responding to a tender has a difficult job on his/her hands if the systems don't exist.

Marketing is the process that helps the firm get onto tender lists (see Chapter two). Ideally, you will have had a period of contact with the client before a tender is issued and know when it is likely to be issued or that it is on its way. Once invited to tender, your planning and selling skills come to the fore. Pitching for work requires a wide variety of marketing and selling skills. It is a very specialised selling situation and sometimes quite formal. However, there are a number of things that you can do to improve your chances of success and this chapter has been designed to act as a guide to those who are preparing a tender for the first time.

It can take a lot of time (which costs money) to prepare a good tender and sometimes large amounts of fees – and your reputation – are at stake. Ideally, you should measure the amount of time you spend on tendering as this is a huge opportunity cost (see Chapter nine on Firm-wide selling issues). Remember, bidding can be scary – but it can also be a great deal of fun. It is rewarding to have worked on and prepared a good tender – even if, at the end of the day, you do not win – you know that you have done your best.

In some respects, responding to an invitation to tender is an exercise in applying just about all your marketing and selling skills in one focused situation. Therefore, many of the ideas and skills already mentioned in this book will have value to you when tendering. However, for completeness, they are all mentioned in this chapter, although you may have to check other chapters in order to get further guidance on specific techniques.

Common mistakes

There are lots of mistakes made frequently by those – both inexperienced and seasoned professionals – who submit tenders. Following the guidance in this chapter will help you avoid many of them. Some of the most commonly occurring problems are:

A lack of preparation

Often a tender is set aside until a few days before the deadline making it difficult to undertake the necessary research, planning, preparation and rapport building with the client. Take immediate action – even if it means passing it on to someone else – as soon as a tender is received. Ideally, your research and marketing efforts will give you advance warning about the arrival of a tender so that you can ensure the relevant resources are available when needed.

Too inward looking

Many firms fall into the easy trap of providing a lot of information about their firm without addressing the specific needs and interests of the client. Even when clients ask for information about the firm, it must be conveyed in an order and manner which is client oriented. Too many tenders have volumes of information explaining every nuance of the tendering firm with no regard to what information might be of interest to the client.

Boilerplate

Some firms always use the same format, material and people in each tender. Year after year they roll out the same old tender document – with a few name changes to reflect the different client. The information is not modified at all to reflect the specific interests of the client. A related problem is failing to change or remove references to former clients who have also received the same tender document in the past.

Lack of team effort

Some firms include their colleagues in other departments and write about their skills, expertise and fees without checking with them first. This results in a lack of internal consultation and teamwork and results in confusion which is painfully obvious to the client. It can sometimes result in inappropriate pricing which can make the work – if won – unprofitable. The problems are compounded where your tender requires you to present people and capabilities in overseas offices or associations. Furthermore, the problems of integration are exasperated in consortium bid situations.

Lack of planning and integration

Each tender, as you will see, is actually a process which starts the moment you are invited to tender and continues long after the client has chosen an adviser. Each stage of the process must be carefully planned and integrated to be effective. Many firms incorrectly see the initial discussions or the written document as separate activities from, say, the oral presentation.

Elements of a competitive tender

There are several stages where client contact (touchpoints) occurs in a competitive tendering situation – in some cases they may all be involved:

- Invitation to tender (ITT or RFP) received from the client – by letter, phone, email or face-to-face.
- Telephone calls, e-mails and letters with the client (e.g. to accept the invitation, to confirm dates, to seek clarification or additional information etc.).
- An informal briefing meeting or site visit with the client.
- A formal briefing meeting with the client.
- A written bid document for the client and its advisors.
- A formal presentation to the client.

- A formal question panel of the client's staff and advisors.

- An informal debriefing with the client by telephone or in person.

Each point of contact with the client during the process needs careful planning and execution. You start to create an impression at the first moment of contact, so the selling process starts here. Expert handling of the apparently 'informal' elements can have a powerful impact on the final decision of the client.

You may find that in very big bids, a shortlist of finalists will be selected from the initial meeting, the written document or the presentation. In such cases, it may be necessary to repeat some of the bid process steps.

A good bid will ensure that all elements – whether on the telephone, in written documents, or in person – reinforce and compliment each other and present a consistent message/theme. The various elements will build upon each other to complete the final case. Remember that a chain is only as good as the weakest link – you will not succeed if you invest all your effort in the formal presentation and neglect the initial contact or the written bid. Similarly, a beautifully prepared document will not compensate for poor preparation, planning and rehearsals for a presentation.

The most important point to remember

As with all marketing and selling activity, the most important point to remember is to adopt the point of view of the client at every possible step. Remember to keep the client in mind at all times – and that clients have both professional and personal needs – different personalities at the client organisation may need and respond to different things: What do they want? What will they buy? How do they view us as a firm? What is most important to them? What are their critical success factors? What do they want to hear? How do they want the information presented? What sort of people are they? How will they react to the pitches from our competitors?

They are interested in solving their problem. At every stage, ask yourself – will the client find this interesting? If in any doubt – leave it out! Also remember that your bid has to meet the needs of a variety of individuals who will make up the decision-making unit (see Chapter four on Buyer behaviour) – so in addition to the corporate needs and concerns you must also consider the individuals' needs and concerns.

The need for a framework

It is important to recognise that you need a framework or checklist within which to prepare for all tenders, no matter how large or small. You usually need to respond quite quickly and often there are many individuals involved – so in all the haste things may be overlooked – therefore the framework ensures you do as much as you can in each bid situation to maximise your chances of success. Not all stages will be appropriate to every bid but you need to consider their relevance in each bid situation – that way you will not omit anything important or overlook a key issue.

Admittedly, some of the success factors are largely out of your control. For example, there is an element of luck relating to the personalities of the selection panel and how they interact with the team you put forward. But there are also many other factors which you can control to ensure that, at best, you win, but at worst, you don't lose as a result of poor preparation.

Sometimes you should break the rules!

Having said you should follow a framework or a process, you should also be prepared to break the rules. There are occasions when things move more swiftly than you anticipated and you may need to leapfrog some stages or processes. The key is to be attuned to the client's needs and to take opportunities when they arise. It has been known for professionals to walk into a first meeting or into a tendering session, expecting a long and drawn out sales process, to respond appropriately to the client's needs and walk away from the meeting with the business.

Using the framework

There are several steps in a successful bid preparation framework. Some steps may be less important or even unnecessary in smaller bids. The steps are as follows:

1   To bid or not to bid?

2   Who will manage the bid preparation?

3   What do you do at initial client contact/meetings?

4   What does the client really want?

5   What selling strategy do you adopt?

6   What price should you quote?

7   How will you do the work if you win?

8   How do you write the bid document?

9   How do you produce and publish the bid document?

10 How do you prepare the oral presentation?

11 When do you ask for the business?

12 What have you learnt?

1 To bid or not to bid?

This may surprise some people as most assume they will attempt to win all tenders. Ideally, your marketing strategy (see Chapter two) will ensure that you only receive the tenders from the sorts of organisations that you want to work for. But when you receive an unexpected invitation to tender you should ask yourself some searching questions:

Do you stand a fair chance of winning?

Is it a level playing field? Is the client impartial or is there an element of 'fait accompli' about the bid? The client may be tendering in order to keep their present advisers on their toes (this sometimes occurs in public sector situations where market testing or compulsory competitive tendering (CCT) is enforced). The client may be trying to get the same advice but at a lower price than they pay at present. You may know that the client is predisposed to a particular firm. A particularly difficult situation occurs when you are asked to re-bid for an existing client.

Are you really able to win and do the work?

Is the area of work one of your strengths, or an area you actively target? The work may relate to an area of the firm that is already very busy or under-resourced. There is nothing more embarrassing and frustrating than winning work that you cannot produce quickly and to the highest quality. Are the relevant people available to help in the preparation and presentation of the bid? It is better not to bid than to bid with a lower quality team than you could field in better circumstances. Clients are unlikely to buy a service from anyone other than those who will be delivering the service.

Is it profitable?

You may not want to increase the amount of work you do in a particular area because it is not profitable. You may be able to win the work only if you heavily discount fees. Discounted fees may also belie your expertise if it is one of the areas where your firm has a strong and leading reputation. There is much debate over offering to do work with little or no profit (or even, in extreme cases, at a loss) in order to 'get a foot in the door' or because there are lots of fee earners around who have little to do. Clients are alert to this and some will select a tenderer for the one piece of unprofitable work with no intention of providing any other work. Some firms offer very low rates to get experience in a market – however, in certain markets (such as health and the public sector) word can get around about the low rates and the firm may find it impossible to raise them at a later date for other clients in the sector.

By accepting work at very low or no profit a number of things might happen:

- The client will always expect the same low fee levels (making later increases difficult).

- The staff working on the matter will become demotivated and more likely to produce less than the highest quality work.

- You may find that you have to decline more profitable work in the future because staff are committed to unprofitable work.

Could you be conflicted out in the future?

If the tender relates to an area of strength there may be conflict situations that prevent the firm from undertaking other work – either now or in the future.

Can you afford to bid?

How much, in both time and out-of-pocket expenditure, will it cost to bid? Are the potential fees attractive enough to risk this investment? Most bids require a large amount of partner time in order to prepare a strong case. These resources may be better deployed on other bids or other fee earning or marketing projects. There may be costs involved in travelling to the client or for research.

Can the client pay?

Can the client afford to pay the amount necessary to ensure you can complete the work profitably? Is the client solvent? Is the client likely to be good at paying their bills promptly?

What would be the consequences of being seen to lose such a bid?

There is more and more press coverage about how major bids are conducted, who participates and the reasons why various firms have lost and won. There are some cases (for example, where you stand little chance of winning) where it may be better not to bid than to be seen to have bid and lost.

What are the prospects for future work with the client if you win this bid?

There may be high fees and a prestigious client but there may be little prospect of follow-on work or an ongoing relationship and the work could conflict you out of other future work.

Is it a reputable organisation? Is it a client that your firm would rather not be associated with? Is it prestigious?

Is it a really prestigious piece of work with great potential for publicity and raising your profile? If so, then the effects of losing a bid could be very damaging as well.

You must consider these questions carefully. Ideally, your firm should have some sort of risk management process (see Chapter nine) to ensure you do not attempt to win work that is not commercially viable or may have negative impacts on your firm. In some cases, a carefully worded decline will put you in a better position with the client than a poor bid. There have been instances where honesty in a decline (e.g. 'The right team is not available at present') has led to a firm being awarded the work at a later date and without having to go through a competitive comparison. Furthermore, if you do not bid on one occasion you may be asked to bid again. If you bid and make a mess of it you will not be invited again. The implications of an unsuccessful bid may go further than the tendering client as word spreads about one spectacular loss.

Another technique you may usefully employ is to try and estimate the chances of winning the tender. You may decide that if there is only a 15% chance of winning the work then the amount of effort involved in bidding is not justified.

2 Who will manage the bid preparation?

From the very beginning, you must be absolutely sure who is responsible for each aspect of the bid preparation. It is best, at the outset, to allocate responsibility for the following aspects of the bid process:

Who has overall responsibility?

This should be a partner who will be the lead partner should you win the work, and one who has the time and expertise available to oversee the whole bid process, which can be a time consuming exercise. One recent bid at a property firm took over 20 meetings over several months and a mountain of documentation to complete, addressing the skills and services of six different departments and five offices – and there were 17 tendering firms.

Who can contribute to the bid preparation?

There are usually a number of people in the firm who can make a valuable contribution to the bid planning or presentation. It will be the job of the partner with overall responsibility to ensure that all these people are identified and consulted early at the initial stages and to ensure that the smaller core team is identified for completing the bid.

Who will liaise with the client?

This is likely to be the person with overall responsibility but sometimes the client may have an existing contact with the firm with whom they would prefer to deal during the initial stages.

Who will research the material required?

A wealth of internal and external information and material must be obtained (see the material on research in Chapter six) – to brief the bidding team, to learn about the client and its market and its likely needs to incorporate into the bid document and presentation and to understand the competition so that an effective positioning and sales strategy can be developed. Some of the research effort can be allocated to less senior members of the bidding team or to information, knowledge management, professional support or business development staff.

Who will write the letter or bid documentation?

It is possible to get different people in the firm to contribute various elements of the document. However, one person needs to co-ordinate who will write what, and when the material must be available. One person must also take responsibility for editing the whole document (or multi-media electronic presentation) into a cohesive whole.

Who will attend the presentation?

There are a number of 'rules of thumb' governing how many and who to take to meetings and presentations (see below). Increasingly, clients request that the more junior members of the team – who will be undertaking the majority of the day-to-day work – attend meetings and presentations.

Who will make up the proposed team to undertake the work?

Those who present must generally be the proposed work team.

Who will lead the presentation?

One person must be responsible for 'chairing' the firm's presentation and discussion at the oral presentation.

Who will take responsibility for rehearsing the speakers?

As well as rehearsing each person attending the presentation and organising a dummy run, it is helpful to have someone outside the core team who can prepare a list of questions and discussion points to test the team's reaction in a dummy bid situation.

Will it be necessary to involve the most senior members of the firm in the bid process?

Often the most senior members of the firm are involved in tenders because it is thought the client will appreciate it. However, there must be a clearly identified role for everyone attending the presentation or appearing on the team. Some feedback indicated that clients were irritated at the 'gratuitous' presence of the senior partner, or that they felt the senior partner prevented younger members of the team from demonstrating their abilities and views.

Who will contact the client to determine the outcome and reasons for success/failure?

Usually this would be the lead partner but if the personal chemistry does not work it is best for someone else to call. Sometimes you obtain a more honest response if someone not involved in the actual tender makes the call.

By addressing these issues, you may find that the people you need are unable to provide the time and input necessary to ensure success, in which case an early decline must be forwarded.

One person must be charged with ensuring that all aspects of the bid preparation progress smoothly and on schedule. An urgent action is to prepare a schedule so that all work on the bid can be completed at the latest by the client's deadline, but ideally a little bit earlier (getting a bid document, CD Rom presentation or electronic material to a client a day or two before the deadline indicates efficiency and keenness). Missing the deadline or requesting an extension is unlikely to help your chances of success and will probably rule you out. In these e-business times, response times can be extremely rapid (e.g. in a recent case the ITT was received on Friday evening and the deadline was 9am the following Monday!) making excellent co-ordination and leadership imperative.

An early action is to arrange a meeting where all the bidding team can get together to 'brainstorm' the key issues to include in the bid and your sales strategy.

3 What do you do at initial client contact meetings?

For larger or more complex bids, you may find you are able to meet with the client to discuss their requirements in more detail before submitting the bid or giving the presentation. If this is not suggested by the client it is always worth asking. Many clients do not offer a briefing meeting but automatically exclude tenderers who do not request it. Alternatively, if the request to the senior person at the organisation is declined you could ask for a meeting with a more junior person instead. This is one way where you can demonstrate keenness and an edge over your competitors. It also gives an additional opportunity to contact the client and obtain other information that may help your bid.

However, such an initial client meeting must be carefully planned as the amount and quality of relevant information you obtain can be critical to your bid's success. In addition, you should be aware that your conduct at such an 'initial' meeting will have a great bearing on the first impression the client has of you and, subsequently, the likelihood of your success.

If the client is unable or unwilling to have an initial briefing meeting you can elicit almost as much information from a carefully planned telephone call. However, you will not benefit from observing 'body language' signals and developing a personal relationship as you would at a face-to-face meeting.

A telephone call must be planned with the same care and forethought as a meeting. Before the meeting or telephone call:

Do some research

(You should also read the material on research in Chapter six).

- **Check the marketing database**: Check the firm's database and/ or intranet and contact those people within your firm who are noted as having contact with, or knowledge of, the client or its competitors.

- **Ask around the firm**: Send an email (or post a note to a bulletin board) to determine if anyone knows about the client organisation or its market. If it is an existing client, read the files. See if there are any instructions you have undertaken for the 'other side' (e.g. pitching to landlords where you have acted for their tenants).

- **Use information, library or knowledge resources**: Check the published and on-line directories both internally and externally to obtain firm details, directors names, turnover, employee details, type of business information, existing advisers, portfolio information and subsidiary relationships. Look at the organisation's website and also the websites of the professional or trade associations to which they may belong. Review the on-line versions of their trade magazines to obtain recent press comment. Contact brokers, investment analysts or journalists who may have insights into their organisation. Obtain a firm listing (there are on-line services to help you do this) with financial statements. Systems commonly available in professional firms include One Source and Mergermarket. Look up information on the people on the panel (their interests, their concerns, their preferences, their role in the decision-making process, their links with other advisers etc.) using directories such as '**Who's Who**', '**Dunn & Bradstreet Directors**' or the Internet.

  Find out about the market the client operates in (you must demonstrate an empathy with their concerns) by checking out relevant sources on the Internet. Find out about the firm's other advisers (e.g. accountants, lawyers, consultants) – you can find this out in publications such as **Hambros** and **Hemmington Scott**. Once you have determined their current advisers, try to find out the reasons they are seeking alternatives and obtain information on the client that has recently appeared in the Press (there are on-line search facilities). Review the trade and technical journals for the client's sector, identify key players, major issues and emerging trends. You should cast your net wide – the broader your knowledge base, the better your chances of identifying something that your competitors have missed. Some firms even commission external research organisations to undertake a thorough review of the tendering organisation and its market, to make this process quicker and more comprehensive.

- **Contact the client organisation**: Obtain an annual report and any other brochures or documents (or web based information) that will give you an insight into the client organisation, its markets, its style, its mission and its aims. Do not limit yourself to documents which have direct relevance to the area of advice sought as all information will help you identify additional needs.

Once you have assembled all the information, prepare a pack which contains all the details but also highlight the key issues and findings that you think will be relevant to the bid. Ensure every member of the bid team has a copy of this briefing document and reads it as quickly as possible.

Read the brief

- Make sure that the invitation to tender and initial instructions from the client have been carefully read and understood. Identify any questions you have on the brief.

- Read any supporting information thoroughly. Highlight any uncertainties or ambiguities, try to work out what they really want and what they are trying to say.

Set objectives

- Make sure you are clear about what you want out of the meeting or telephone call beforehand and concentrate on achieving these things.

Prepare questions

- Prepare a list of questions and grade them according to their importance, otherwise you may find that time constraints prevent you from getting to the bottom of your list and the most important questions. Try to formulate open ended questions (How? What? Why?), rather than closed questions that can be answered with a simple 'Yes' or 'No' (see Chapter six for material on questioning techniques and also Chapter five on SPIN®).

Ask questions

- If you have secured a meeting, arrange for one person to ask the questions and another person to take notes, this way you can maintain eye contact and observe body language (see Chapter six for information on non-verbal communication).

- When you ask questions, make sure you listen to the answers and do not attempt to answer the questions for the client. Make sure you spend at least 50% of the time listening (see Chapter six for material on active listening). Do not be afraid of pauses – the client may need time to think.

- Think carefully about whether you can ask who else is bidding and whether the client has a budget in mind for the work. Determining the number of copies required of any documents or CD ROMs will tell you how many people are involved in the decision-making process.

Sell yourself

- By asking relevant, informed questions you can score points with the client. Only by careful research can you be fully prepared to ask appropriate questions. Be confident and friendly. Make sure you know enough about the client, their market and their bid to demonstrate credibility. Deal positively with any questions they ask and have a strategy for dealing with any questions which you are unable to answer. Think whether you will want to send them any information (for example, booklets on related subjects or e-mails containing pages from your intranet) in advance to lay the foundations of your case.

Build rapport

- Think about the person you are speaking to. Try to adjust to their style and personality. Try to develop a rapport (see Chapter four for information on empathy and personality types and Chapter six for material on conversational skills).

- Make sure you deal with any receptionists and secretaries at the client organisation with care. They are effectively 'gatekeepers' and you need them on your side, so create a good impression (see the decision-making unit in Chapter four).

You should always make sure that at least one member of the bidding team has visited the client's premises and any other relevant sites. By actually going to the client's premises you will achieve a number of things:

- You will demonstrate your interest and initiative.
- You have a chance to obtain extra information.
- You have a chance to identify any issues that are not apparent from the briefing.
- You have a chance to create a good impression with anyone you meet while visiting.
- You have a chance of discovering an inside track. Remember though that an informal site visit is still a selling situation. You only have one chance to make a good impression!

4 What does the client really want?

A common mistake is to notice one element that you are good at in the initial brief and to go gung-ho into preparing your case on that basis. Read and digest **all** the information they have provided and compare this with all the information you have collected during your research and preliminary meetings and discussions.

Forget for a moment what you want to sell to the client – ask yourself what the client is asking for and what they really need. What do they want to buy? Often, there is a 'hidden agenda' in that the client is keeping back, either deliberately or unintentionally, important information. Then think about what you can sell them.

Think beyond the brief

In essence, they have a problem for which you must come up with the best, and only, solution. Ask as many colleagues as possible about the likely needs of the client. Organise a 'brainstorm' to identify other needs or issues that the client may have. Imagine what issues keep the directors of the tendering company awake at night. Think about other clients in the same market. Think about the commercial issues facing all companies in the client's industry sector. Think about each member of the client organisation's views and their perceptions of professional advisers. Imagine that you are the client and consider what would most impress or concern you. At the end of the day, all tendering firms will be responding to the client's written or stated requirements – your task is to uncover as many new and additional needs that they may have that only you can meet.

Their decision criteria

An important part of this thought process is obtaining an understanding of the selection criteria to be used by the client (see Chapter four for further information about buying criteria). Think about the relative importance the client will attach to each of the following:

- Members (size, sex, race, age and seniority) of the proposed team
- Written/electronic bid document.
- Presentation/discussion.
- Understanding of their requirements.
- Enthusiasm/youth/similarity to the client's team.
- Adherence to their initial instructions.
- Track record in the area.
- Specialist expertise you are offering.
- The way you will tackle the job (e.g. methodology, process, computer systems etc.).
- Reputation of the firm.
- Price.

- Innovative ideas or problem-solving skills.

- Speed with which you can act.

- Use of technology.

- Added value that you can provide.

Many clients will have decided in advance on their selection criteria. However, they may not be aware of unconscious criteria such as the whiteness of the shirts of your team, the brightness of their smiles, the 'hunger' you demonstrate for the work, the professionalism of your team and the way you speak. Surprisingly, the price is often not a key criteria in the selection procedure.

You should remember that not all decisions will be based on rational criteria. Think, for example, about the reassurance and greater certainty buyers will obtain from choosing a big 'brand' name. Consider too that although many pitching organisations will have rated and weighted each tendered against rational and objective criteria – the final decision may well be an irrational or emotional decision based on past allegiances, how their decision might be perceived by their colleagues, undue regard for the opinions of influencers or purely relationship issues such as their preference for a particular group of individuals over others.

5 What selling strategy should you adopt?

It is important to consider why you were asked to bid. If the client has perceptions about the firm then you must be sure you understand why they have asked you to bid, what they perceive as your particular strengths (and weaknesses) and respond accordingly.

You should, by now, know what the client wants and what you are intending to sell to them. Now you need to decide how you are going to sell to them – the selling strategy. The strategy you adopt will depend on many factors, for example, the nature of the client organisation, the strength of your case, the team you are putting forward and the likely strategies of your competitors.

There are two stages in developing the selling strategy:

1 What is our case?

Do a SWOT (Strengths, Weaknesses, Opportunities, Threats) analysis. What strengths do you have? What strengths do the competing bidders have? Why are you different/better than the other bidders? Are you offering a particularly competitive price? Are you providing any value-added service? Why should the client choose you? What benefits will they obtain? What can they get from you that they cannot get from other firms? For example, you could show that you have taken a lot of time and effort to research their needs or that you have particular experience in their problem/market. You may have identified additional issues that may prove important to them or you may have a particularly innovative solution. Alternatively, you may have invested in technology and have developed a particularly attractive knowledge-base or computer based tool that the client would find valuable. Increasingly, the prospect of a strategic alliance or partnership arrangement is attractive to clients. If there is no difference between your bid and those of your competitors in effect you are offering a commodity service and price will dictate the outcome (see below on pricing).

When it comes to considering how you position yourself against your competitors you may wish to complete a table similar to the following:

COMPETITOR	EXISTING RELATIONSHIP	SIZE OF SPECIALIST TEAM	TRACK RECORD	RELATED CLIENTS	TECHNOLOGY SOLUTIONS	TOTAL
Our firm	2	8	9	7	2	28
Competitor A	10	6	2	4	9	31
Competitor B	6	2	6	9	9	32

2 How do you present your case?

You may have control over the way in which you present your case. You may be able to choose an informal or formal meeting, a detailed written bid document or a brief letter, a formal or informal presentation, the client premises or your premises for meetings etc. The use of visual aids, from simple flip charts to elaborate multi-media presentations, must be carefully considered. (Note: If you intend to use audio-visuals make sure that the client has the necessary equipment and that it is set up and working before the presentation.) You should think carefully what the individuals would expect and be most comfortable with and you should consider how your presentation will be compared against the competitors.

THE FIRM'S OVERALL POSITIONING

In many cases your key strength will be the overall positioning of the firm as a leader in key areas of expertise and/or your in-depth knowledge of the relevant areas of the market. Whatever strategy you adopt in your tender should be consistent with your overall positioning.

UNIQUE SELLING PROPOSITION (USP)

The key to an effective strategy is to position yourself in a unique way that the other tenderers cannot match – making you the only and obvious choice. By careful management of the tendering process you can set the agenda and criteria against which the client will measure all tenders. (The material on persuading in Chapter six may assist here.)

PROFESSIONAL OR 'LAYMAN'?

An important consideration when preparing your strategy is the extent to which those on the selection panel are technically qualified as professionals. The way you sell yourself to an in-house professional and the types of questions and concerns they may have will be quite different to those from a non-professional buyer. Your strategy and your whole approach needs to be modified to address this point. Some decisions will be made by mixed professional and laymen panels.

You should also remember the material on the decision-making unit (Chapter four).

6 What price should you quote?

Strategic pricing policy is set within the context of your business or marketing plan (see Chapter two). Tactical pricing is what you manipulate in order to achieve a particular sale. Make sure you are clear about what you are manipulating and why.

Most professional firms prefer to operate on a percentage fee or time charged basis. Yet increasingly clients require fixed price estimates or arrangements where they have more certainty or flexibility in the pricing. If everything else amongst competing firms is equal (i.e. you are not differentiated and the client is purchasing a commodity), price will be the deciding factor. Much of this book is designed to ensure that your proposal is different from the competition but pricing will remain the one area most likely to be raised for discussion at the presentation.

Psychology of pricing

There are a number of important principles that many people apply when it comes to pricing. Often they will ignore both the most expensive and the cheapest prices, and opt for one in the middle range (unless you explain why your price is particularly high or low). People react nervously to large, round numbers (e.g. £197,756 will feel more credible than £200,000 unless you have indicated that you have rounded down). People tend to react more positively when they can see a breakdown of the price and therefore feel able to manipulate or negotiate specific elements.

Cost versus price

There are two elements involved in preparing your estimate. First, determine the likely cost of doing the work (by using the standard fee rates for each member of the team). Second, assess how much you will charge the client (this will depend on the client's perception of your value and the importance of the work to them) and the way you will make the charge (i.e. billing and payment methods). The two issues are related but quite separate. Until you know exactly how much it will cost it will be difficult to determine what profit margins are involved and what leeway you have to either uplift or discount the price. Some firms maintain databases which show the actual costs of similar past jobs so that the costing process is very quick and accurate.

You need to cost out the work in as much detail as possible – even if this information is not presented in the document or at the presentation. This may require a considerable amount of information from the client about volumes, frequency etc. Spending a significant amount of time working through how you will do the work and how much time it will take, will have the added advantage of giving you the confidence to show that you really know what is involved in the project and to talk about the fees.

A common issue for professional services is working out how to charge for the different members of the team or whether to suggest blended rates. Again, try to view this from the client's point of view – they may be prepared to pay a lot for one especially experienced individual but very little for a junior member of the team. Make sure you build in contingencies too.

Professional buyers may prefer to see a time based price – they can then use their professional judgement to assess whether the fees are reasonable. Lay clients may find more comfort in a fixed fee or project price.

If your solution contains significant value from knowledge systems, access to information or shared developments then it is important that your price reflects your investment in this as well as the perceived value to the client of this intellectual property. Pricing information based services is addressed in a book by Ross Dawson.

Premium prices v discounts

Are you offering a premium added value service where you have a particularly strong team with rather rare expertise? If so, it would be inadvisable to quote a low, highly discounted rate for such expertise – it negates the strength of your expertise. In such instances it may be possible to uplift the prices. Clients often equate price with quality, and a low price might suggest low quality.

A discount is supposed to be an incentive to purchase, yet clients may view discounts with suspicion. When offering discounts (such as for large volumes of work for a specific period) think in terms of small increments such as 2.75% or 3.25%, rather than large rounded numbers.

Is there a large volume of low level work where you are prepared to offer discounts? There may be ways in which you can offset the high cost of your premium expertise and work by offering to undertake more routine matters at a lower rate.

Think how important the work is to the client (e.g. strategic impact) to determine their views on value and risk.

Fixed rate and task rates

Showing fee rates of team members is rarely sufficient – it forces the client to make naive comparisons (it may take only an hour for a very senior and experienced person to do something that a less experienced person would spend days on). Commercial advice providing real business advantage is undersold on an hourly rate.

Retainers

If the tender is for an ongoing and regularly used service – such as management accounts, annual audits, ongoing employment support or some form of outsourcing arrangement then it may be necessary to provide an annual or quarterly retainer based on assumptions about the anticipated levels of work. In such situations it will be important to specify how volumes far exceeding those anticipated will be dealt with. It may be necessary to be very specific about additional costs that fall outside the retainer arrangement. Details of how the retainer may be modified should be included in the documentation.

Shared risk and abortives

It is increasingly common for clients to expect their advisers to share some of the risk and, sometimes, to share in the rewards. Try to give an indication of the amount of work involved and break it down into the various stages or types of work – this also demonstrates that you have seriously considered how you will do the work if you win it. If you can't give a fixed fee or percentage for the whole transaction then provide estimates for specific tasks or stages and provide fee rates for the other work.

Remember that if the client is not a trained professional they may not know what steps are involved or the potential difficulties in what would appear to be a simple and straightforward transaction. Try to educate the client as to why the percentage, fee rates or fixed fees are at the levels that they are.

If you are unable to provide a fixed(ish) fee – offer a range (upper and lower rates) and explain the assumptions used. Alternatively, offer fixed fees for those elements you can estimate and hourly or daily rates for other work.

Some clients may expect a Conditional Fee Arrangement (CFA) where the payment depends on the outcome achieved. Ensure you have experience in these sorts of arrangements and that you have assessed the risk factors carefully.

For barristers, it may be necessary to provide both a trial or brief fee and a range of fees depending on whether and at what stage the case may settle.

Shared development costs

Where technology or know-how systems are a key element of the work being undertaken, you may wish to partially contribute to the investment in doing the work if it is possible for you to re-use that work with other clients. If this is the case then it is important that you make this clear in the fee proposals and ensure that you have the necessary contractual arrangements to allow you to re-use and re-charge for the work with other clients.

Competitor pricing

Even if you are not going to base your prices on those of competitors (if you are able to determine these) you should consider how others may price the work. If you suspect that you are either going to be way above or below the competing bids this must be addressed in the document and explained.

Demonstrate real added value

An important way to support the fees you propose is to identify the added value that you will bring to the client – for example, have you got contacts that would help them? Can you provide services that other firms cannot match? Do you possess unusual sector/industry experience? Can you offer free briefing or training to their staff on critical issues? Can they access your research and information services? Do you have a valuable knowledge base or electronic service delivery mechanism? Can you offer free briefing to your or their staff to reduce the learning curve and speed up the work? Can you provide a senior or junior member of the team on secondment at their premises? You may have included a client care partner in the team, in which case you are unlikely to charge for their time in this role – ensure that any 'free' services are presented as such.

Other techniques

Pricing models are evolving all the time in response to client needs. It is important that you keep up-to-date with your competitors' proposals so that your firm does not fall behind in offering outdated pricing and billing models. Discounts for early payment and other devices might be employed to offset seemingly high rates or fixed fees. Ideally, you should learn to offer additional services or benefits instead of price reductions when trying to win business.

At the presentation you may be asked to talk through the fees or estimates in detail. Be prepared to do this with confidence. (Some professionals teach their younger staff to look in the mirror and say 'I am worth £200 an hour'!). Clients are unsettled by people who look nervous or uncomfortable when discussing fees. Yet a discussion about price is a positive sign! When the client is discussing price they are signalling to you that they want your solution and need only address the price in order to proceed. Decide in advance whether you are going to offer additional 'incentives' having once put a figure in the written document. Clients often 'test' the chosen firm by seeing if there is more 'discount' to be obtained. See the material on negotiation in Chapter six.

7 How will you do the work if you win?

Educate the client

An important element of the written bid is demonstrating to the client how you will tackle the work if you win. In some cases you are educating the client or, at least, helping them appreciate what must be done and why. Help them see the various stages, the decision points, the potential difficulties, the potential delays or problems, the time scales, the various outcomes and the 'outputs' (i.e. tangible results such as contracts, completions, books, planning applications etc.) of each stage. This is part of making an intangible service more tangible.

The role of each member of the team

You may need specific individuals to undertake particular areas of the work. Make sure it is clear why each individual is involved and their particular tasks, contribution and responsibilities. Without boring the client, help them understand the various issues and tasks that must be tackled.

The size of the team

Take care in deciding the size of your team. Some clients may consider a large team reassuring, in that all the specialist expertise is available immediately. Other clients may be concerned about the cost of a large team and co-ordination issues. Think carefully about the composition of the team in terms of partners and other professionals and support staff – balance the cost of seniority and expertise and the time of junior and relatively inexperienced staff.

A project plan

Breaking the work into a coherent work plan with stages and time scales etc. can be reassuring to the client who will know that you understand what is involved and are ready to get working on the project straightaway. Some firms include detailed project charts in their tenders – be careful not to overload the client with too much information, just enough to reassure and inspire confidence.

Quality and client care

There should always be one team leader/co-ordinator (e.g. account partner) identified so that the client knows they have one point of contact. You should also consider who you should propose as the relationship or client care partner (a separate point of contact, an additional communication channel and someone with overall responsibility for the quality of the work you do). The client care partner may be available also for senior level meetings and for informal 'audit' meetings where the client can talk about how well (or not) you're providing the service they require (see Chapter eight on Account management).

Innovate

Decide whether there is an opportunity to offer a fresh and innovative approach that will differentiate you from the other bidders. Do you have established methodologies, procedures or checklists that will mean you can complete the work more easily, quickly or cheaply than any other firm? Do you have a knowledge system that confers an advantage? Can you offer case studies that show how you have tackled similar projects for other clients? Do you have a software system that will enable the client to do significant aspects of the work themselves?

Have you thought about a particularly novel or unusual approach to tackle some or all of the client's needs? Does this innovation confer additional benefits to the client in terms of speed, cost or competitive advantage?

Demonstrate you are already 'on the job' mentally

Providing detailed information about how you will do the work does two things for the client. First, it shows that you have the expertise and experience to know what must be done and when – this gives the client reassurance that you are able to do the work and reduces their concerns about risk and uncertainty. Second, it suggests to the client that you have already made the transition and (without appearing to be arrogant) that you are psychologically already doing the work and therefore ahead of the other bidders.

Make sure that the amount of work outlined 'tallies' with the fee level quoted. If you are quoting high fees for rare expertise, or high fees for a large amount of research, then make sure the client understands this.

8 How do you write the bid document?

From the steps so far you should have a number of ideas to write down. Sometimes, clients need only a short letter confirming the main points but more usually you are required to put together a more substantial document (this may be in electronic form).

The first step before putting pen to paper (or fingers to keyboard) is to think about the structure of the bid document. Although there are no hard and fast rules, typical headings of a written bid might be:

- Covering letter.
- Contents.
- Executive summary.
- Introduction/scene setting.
- The client's requirements.
- Other issues identified.
- How your firm will meet the requirements.
- How the job will be tackled.
- Why your firm?
- Your past experience.
- Your team.
- Costs and timescales.
- The firm's client care and quality policies.
- General information about the firm.

As a general rule of thumb, the information most specific and important to the client should be at the start and the material (if any) that is general about your firm should be closest to the end.

Amount of detail

The amount of detail contained in the written submission will depend on several factors. You must know to what extent the document will be used as a basis for selection. It will present your case in your absence, so it should answer as many potential questions as possible. It must address any potential objections the client may have. It must contain the same theme and key points as the material you have and will present personally. Different people within the decision-making unit (see Chapter four) will need different types and amounts of infor:nation. Presenting your tender in electronic format – and with a web browser facility – will allow individuals to drill down to the level of information they require.

Consistent style

You should maintain a consistent writing style throughout. This may mean considerable rewriting and checking where technical sections have been written by different individuals. Obviously, at least one partner should see the final document and one person who has not been involved in the bid discussions should be asked to review the document objectively. You must adhere to your firm's house-style and corporate identity.

Demonstrate knowledge

You need to show that you have an in-depth knowledge of the client's organisation, industry and issues and that you know the subject so well that you can even raise other issues or potential concerns that the client may not yet have thought of. You need to also indicate that you have thought long and hard about their stated and unstated needs. If you can raise other issues than those mentioned in the invitation to tender you are 'setting the agenda' for the appraisal of other bidders, who may not have considered these 'extra' issues or shown that they can handle them.

Plain and simple language

Avoid technical words and jargon unless they are required because the decision-makers are qualified professionals themselves who are seeking purely technical expertise. Use short sentences as they are easier to understand and quicker to read. It is more than likely that at least part of your readership will not be professionally qualified. Clients often say that they can determine a real expert in the way that they explain complex ideas and jargon in a simple and concise way. Lots of rambling explanations and references to other material often indicates to the client that the writer has summarised their research into a subject they knew little about before preparing the tender!

Benefits and differentiators

Remember this is a selling document. Keep in mind the readers' point of view and interests. Make sure all the selling messages are there, integrated into the written content. This includes the benefits (see Chapter six on Persuading), the differentiators and the credibility factors.

Use of existing material

Never incorporate standard 'boilerplate' material without carefully editing and tailoring it to the particular client's needs. If you do use pre-written material, make sure it is up-to-date and correct. If you use material from an earlier bid, find out whether the bid was successful and the reasons why. This is particularly important with CVs and biographies that should always be modified to reflect the needs of the particular bid. If ever in doubt as to whether something should be included, leave it out.

Client names and references

There is much debate about whether to include client names in tenders or not. If you do include names, you should obtain permission from each client before including their name if your professional body requires it. If you offer references you must check that the nominated clients are happy to take a call and that they will give an honest and positive response if called.

Positive tone

Consider the 'tone' of the document. Do you sound complacent or defeatist? Do you sound as if you are bored or awed about the project? Do you sound as if you are really keen for the work? Can sentences be re-phrased to sound more positive? (For example, 'If we were successful we would propose...' converts to 'We propose...').

Client focus

Review the use of 'we' in the document. The client is not primarily concerned with 'we' (your firm) – the client is concerned with 'you' (the client). Avoid using 'we' to start paragraphs and sentences. This means the emphasis must be on benefits or solutions rather than features (see Chapter six on Persuading). If you wish to include a point about something you do or something you have, start the sentence with something that concerns the client. For example 'You have indicated that you are keen to keep one central point of control, for this reason we have identified partner A as the main point of contact who will report to director B each month on the progress of all matters...'.

Proof reading

There are a number of things to watch for when proof reading the document (for example the consistent use of upper and lower case, the consistent use of house-style etc.). Obviously you should check that there are no typing errors, that the client's name is spelt correctly (I promise you that I have seen examples of tenders where the clients name or the names of individuals are spelt incorrectly!) and that the grammar is correct.

Enthusiasm

Remember that somewhere you must thank the client for the opportunity to bid. Thank any of the client's staff who have helped you prepare the bid and stress your keenness, enthusiasm and ability to undertake the work. This may be included in the covering letter (which should be bound into the document to avoid the letter and the document being separated).

Make sure the document is easy to read and interesting from the client's point of view. Does every paragraph really pass the 'So what does this mean to me the client?' test?

9 How do you produce and publish the bid document?

The content of the written bid is important, but so is the way the material is presented. Remember the rules of human perception in terms of what is most likely to attract their eye: images of people's eyes, images of people, images of objects, headings, signatures and postscripts, text containing the recipient's name and familiar numbers and short positive words.

Often the written bid is not read in detail, but you can be sure that the way in which the document is presented will always be noted. Weak presentation can lose the bid for you. Consider the client's reaction to the way the final document looks – glossy and printed may appear expensive to some clients, a full colour multi-media searchable CD ROM may deter more traditional clients. A three page letter may look inadequate if other bidders have submitted hefty bound documents – alternatively, the client may appreciate the brevity and focus. You need to decide whether you will use your own desk top publishing skills (DTP), the services of external designers and printers, or the use of specialist electronic and multi-media producers, or a combination of methods. Each method has its own advantages and disadvantages in terms of cost and time.

Non-text content

Discuss what tables, flow charts, photographs, movies, animations or other diagrams (e.g. the organisation of the team, the way the firm is organised, illustrated case studies, how the work will be tackled) can be incorporated. In addition to breaking up blocks of text, diagrams convey messages in a different way – perhaps making it easier for the client to assimilate. You may want to consider including photographs or video clips of the main members of the team, this aids recognition at meetings and assists later recall of any oral points you may have made. Increasingly, new technology allows you to obtain and create interesting and relevant images which will help differentiate your bid from its competitors. The digital camera and on-line photo libraries come into their own here! (But take care with copyright and reproduction licence fees.)

Translations

If you are bidding to a foreign or international client, it may be advisable to consider translating the whole or parts of the bid. You could consider having the English words facing a page of the same text in a different language. It is, however, much easier to do this in electronic versions where the reader can select their preferred language. On all occasions use professional, technically experienced translators who ideally speak the language as their mother tongue. This will ensure that it sounds as natural as possible. However, these are expensive and there will also be problems with checking text changes if you do not have the in-house language skills.

Electronic documents

Sometimes you may need to submit an electronic document – either because the client has requested it in this format or because of time and distance issues. Electronic documents come in two broad categories: As printed and web enabled. Using Adobe Acrobat or PDF files means that you obtain an electronic version of the way a properly designed and printed document might appear, but on the screen. It is a static document that allows the client only to scroll through in the order prepared or printed.

A web enabled document (i.e. uses a browser) provides an environment where the client can select the order and information that is of relevance – in effect, the document is produced as a mini private website. This is particularly attractive where you have a large volume of information to convey, where there are libraries of reference material or staff biographies, or where the assessing individuals have very different interests. It allows you to provide search engines and to incorporate dynamic materials (e.g. animations of processes). However, you need professional assistance in developing these documents to ensure that the client can access the information they need – in the format they need – quickly.

10 How do you prepare the oral presentation?

Some bids require you to make a formal presentation to a selection panel. In other situations you may choose the particular type of presentation you provide. You must prepare, plan and rehearse your presentation thoroughly as it is usually the most important stage of the selection process. Sometimes, the decision may have already been made and your task is simply not to ruin the strong position you have built with the written submission.

Check feedback

Check whether you have any feedback from earlier meetings or the written bid. Find out if the client latched onto any particular idea or person. Find out if the client is particularly interested in any point(s) you have raised. Obviously, the closer your presentation matches their interests, the more successful it will be. Ask the clients what they expect to achieve from the presentation and if there are any particular points they want to be covered in depth.

Agree who will attend

You must decide carefully who from the team will actually participate in the presentation. Some panels may want to see the junior members of the team taking part, yet you may want the most senior members of the practice to present the firm's case. However, you should not outnumber the client's team at the presentation without a very good reason.

Identify the key points

Decide on the main points to include in the presentation. You must not simply regurgitate all the material in the written bid. Select the most important points (from the client's point of view) and those which enable you to present the strongest case for your firm.

Make sure you do not try to present too much information in the time available. It is better to concentrate on one or two key messages or issues, as there is more likelihood that these will be understood and remembered.

Plan your use of time

It is important that you know in advance how much time the client expects the presentation to last. You should leave ample time for the client to ask questions and aim to leave at least five minutes before your allotted time is up (it is alright to stay if the client requests it). There is nothing more embarrassing than the client having to ask you to leave before you are finished followed by a disorganised gathering of papers and rushing out of the room. Make sure you have an agenda of some kind – which you should check with the client in case they wish to cover different topics. You should plan to have each member of your team talk for at least a few minutes. As a rule of thumb, with an hour allocated your team should not present for more than 20 minutes – the aim is to get the client talking as much as possible. Sometimes, the adage 'less is more' should be remembered. If the client is satisfied with your presentation after only, say, 20 minutes of your hour, do not feel compelled to stay there until your time allocation has finished – a client could have made up their mind and additional input from you in this case could 'unsell'.

Prepare introductions

Make sure the person 'chairing' the presentation can introduce each member of the team and make a short introduction. Every person attending the presentation must have something to say – ideally about their particular area of expertise or the aspects of the client's project they will be managing. It is important that you allow the client to introduce their team – to explain their different roles and interests.

Visual aids

The use of visual aids is sometimes controversial. There are associated difficulties with using videos, slides, CD ROMs or Powerpoint presentations, such as the need to check equipment beforehand, the production time required and the difficulty in gaining access to client premises to rehearse with their equipment. The use of visual aids does add an element of formality that you may wish to avoid. Some visual aids – like videos – can take a valuable amount of time that might be better spent talking.

Some members of your team may feel uncomfortable or be inexperienced in using audio-visual aids or electronic presentations. If you do use aids, you must prepare their content and presentation carefully. You must also be prepared for disasters such as power cuts, equipment failure, drinks splashed on laptops, projector bulbs breaking, failing telecommunication connections etc. However, if all bidders use electronic presentations you have a chance to differentiate your team by using a 'chat round the table' approach. One recent team won a major tender partly because they used no electronic kit but had prepared some innovative A1 sized boards from which they tore off velcro strips at key points – the clients loved this low tech but highly innovative and entertaining approach. It certainly differentiated the team!

Rehearse a lot

Whether or not you are using audio-visual aids, and whether or not you are giving a formal presentation you must rehearse. There should be at least one rehearsal with all members of the presentation team present. You should invite an 'uninvolved' audience of colleagues as their questions will be similar to those asked by the client. Take care with your own body language and observing theirs (see Chapter six on non-verbal communication). You may wish to provide handouts of copies of the slides. A further aid to preparing and rehearsing are training videos. You can arrange to video your 'performance' to critically review at a later stage. You can practise working with any audio-visuals you may have and become familiar with the audio-visual or computer equipment.

'Dummy' panels

You may also wish to do a 'dummy run' with a pretend client panel. Someone should brief and prepare the dummy panel so that you cover as many of the potential problems and opportunities that you are likely to face with the client. The dummy panel will allow you to rehearse in as close a manner as possible to the actual event and they will be able to guide you on which areas of your presentation that could be improved.

Identify all possible questions that might be asked

A critical element of the presentation will be the way you handle questions. You will need to think in advance of all the possible questions the client will ask and prepare confident, clear and concise answers. The most critical question you should be prepared to answer is "Why should we appoint your firm?". Sometimes clients will ask how your approach differs from that of your competitors. This is a tough question as you must not be seen to criticise the competition although it is wise to show that you have a confident enough grasp of how you compare to make some comment. My advise is to focus on the positive along the lines of "Well, we are not in a position to comment in detail on what our competitors are saying – however, taking past client experience into account we know that the investment we have made in developing the securitisation extranet service has been valued by clients as a way to reduce their dependency on...". Decide who will chair the discussion and field questions in each area. Decide how to deal with difficult questions and what will happen if you are unable to answer a question. Prepare a list of your own questions, so that if questions from the client are not forthcoming, you can break the ice and there is no embarrassing silence.

Prepare a list of questions for them

It is good practice to prepare a list of questions to ask the client at the presentation. This gives you an opportunity to demonstrate your knowledge and grasp of the issues, as well as showing an intelligent interest in their organisation and concerns. Many clients offer tenderers the opportunity to ask questions at the end and it is very embarrassing if you do not have any.

Take care with the small talk

As you arrive and meet the client there will be a short period of informal small talk. This is likely to be repeated at the end of the session as well. It is vitally important that you are able to convey a positive impression through the small talk, although some personalities will be resistant to small talk that appears too personal or trivial. Refer to the material on conversation skills and networking in Chapter six.

Take care with introductions and seating arrangements

If there is a large number of people at the meeting it may be inappropriate (and difficult logistically) for everyone to shake hands with everyone else. Also, if you are offered a choice of seats try to avoid the 'them versus us' confrontational seating of all their guys on one side of the table and all your guys on the other. However, if mixed seating is possible you will need to take extra care with eye contact and cueing (see Non-verbal communication in Chapter six).

Adjust to match the style of the 'audience'

Whatever you have researched and rehearsed, you are unlikely to have met all the people until the time of the presentation. People have very different styles of doing business and relating to other people. It is important that you match their personalities and moods as much as possible (see Chapter four on Buyer behaviour).

Aim for interaction rather than presentation

The concentration span for most people is quite limited, so the more time you spend interacting with the audience (rather than presenting or lecturing) the better. If the client wants to discuss one point in detail, do not be afraid to abandon some or all of the planned presentation material. For example, if you have an hour in total, your formal presentation should take no more than about 20 minutes – the bulk of the time should be asking and answering questions and building a rapport through interaction.

Although it is termed a presentation, some of the most successful 'presentations' are where the formally presented material is kept to a minimum and the majority of the time is spent talking with the client or working through some aspect of the project. The client needs an opportunity to get to know you as people and to feel how it would be if you were actually working together.

First or last?

Remember in competitive situations the client has had to sit through a number of similar presentations, so if you can make yours different or more memorable then this will be in your favour. Be aware of the primacy and recency effects also. This is very important if you are one of the last presentations they will see – they will be weary at this point and many of their questions may have been 'dictated' by previous pitches – however, if you raise points that others cannot respond to it will set you in good stead. If you are the first presentation they see they are unlikely to be 'in the swing' of the pitch process and it may be a little awkward – however, by going first you have the opportunity to set the standards and questions against which the others will be judged. However, any additional points you have raised will then be mentioned to subsequent bidders so your edge may be reduced.

Be ready to abandon your plans

No matter how well you prepare and rehearse, be prepared to abandon everything if the client indicates this is appropriate. Watch for signs of specific interest, boredom or impatience. Know what non-verbal clues mean 'hurry up' or 'please explain in more detail' or 'I want to speak/ask a question' (see non-verbal communication in Chapter six). You can see if one member of the panel is feeling excluded or unhappy and adjust your behaviour to include them.

Close on a 'high'

As well as trying to retain control over the way the presentation and discussion goes, you should also try to control how the presentation ends. The chairperson should watch the time and alert the client when the allotted time is almost over. Summarise the key points, thank them for the opportunity to bid and stress concisely why your firm should be their choice. Try to end on a strong positive point rather than letting the discussion just drift away. Asking whether they need any additional help or information, or asking when the next step/decision will take place, is a good way to end.

As soon as you have finished your presentation, compare notes with the others who were present to see how you think you fared. If you think the client was confused or missed a point there is no reason why you can't make a short call immediately afterwards.

There is further information about presentation skills in Chapter six.

11 When do you ask for the business?

Do not be afraid of stating your desire to win the work. Do not be afraid to be enthusiastic. Remember to actually ask for the work (see Closing in Chapter six). There is a natural fear of rejection and a natural fear of appearing 'too pushy', which must be overcome. Client feedback indicates that bidders sometimes appear arrogant, complacent or 'not hungry enough' for the work.

The timing of the question is quite important. The client may decide at any time during initial meetings, during a telephone conversation or half way through a presentation that you will win (or lose) the bid. They will usually give some sign (perhaps using body language) or they may ask a direct question relating to a specific point on which their decision hangs. Do not be afraid to stop at this point and ask questions. Many people adhere rigidly to what they have rehearsed, even though the client is clearly showing signs that no more is necessary, or that they wish to spend more time on a particular point. React to what the client wants.

The client may raise objections (see Chapter six on Selling skills). Objections should not be feared – they are often an indication that more information or clarification is required. These can be real objections ('We simply cannot afford you') or false ones. False objections may hide a real objection that the client cannot express (for example, they do not like the personality of a team member). Try to work out the real objection and resolve it. This often involves asking them questions carefully. Do not feel you have failed, deal constructively with the objection and you may recover the situation. Some panels may raise objections to test your reaction under pressure (i.e. an essential part of the selection process) and to see how you operate as a team.

12 What have you learnt?

Immediately after the presentation or panel discussion, have a short debrief with all the staff involved. Obtain the views of everyone present to assess where you were strong and weak, whether the client understands your strengths and case, whether there was any disagreement between members of the panel, who seemed to ask most questions and exert most influence etc. Sometimes you may need to make a quick call after the presentation to check that the client fully understood a point, or to provide information they requested that you were unable to provide at the time.

If you have not heard the outcome by the time indicated that a decision would be taken, phone up and ask.

You (or someone else) must contact the client to determine the reasons for winning or losing a tender. You have put a lot of work and effort into preparing a bid and most clients recognise this and are happy to provide quite a detailed response on how your tender could have been improved, or where others offered or presented things differently. A client is more likely to provide an honest opinion if they are not talking to the individuals who participated, so you may wish to ask another partner or the marketing director to make this call if you were unsuccessful.

You should always ask the client the reasons for success as this input can be used to ensure success at future bids. Most firms keep a log of all major pitches and the reasons for winning and losing bids, so that all your experience can be used to ensure future success and that you identify any reoccurring problems (for example, your pricing always being too high) as early as possible. However, be aware that if a client is uncomfortable telling you that the reason you lost is due to a particular partner or a real weakness in your proposals, they will tend to blame 'price' as a way to avoid embarrassment.

Even if you do not win, do not lose heart, sometimes the chosen team do not live up to expectations and the clients may ask you to talk again. Research shows clients sometimes feel dissatisfied around five and nine months after their chosen firm has been appointed. A well timed call to see how things are going can 'keep the door open' for future contact. Even if you lose the specific tender, if you have performed well and keep in touch the client may approach you again in the future and/or recommend you to other clients.

If you do win, remember you are at the start of a relationship and you must keep working very hard to exceed the expectations that the client now has. It is helpful to think of all client relationships – no matter how well-established and long standing – as 'one long competitive tender'. The next chapter, on account management, shows how the relationship can be developed.

EIGHT
Account management

ROADMAP

This chapter is in two parts. The first part considers the need for a structured approach to account management (sometimes referred to as CRM – Client Relationship Management) and considers the objectives and benefits of such a system. It provides an overview of the account management process. The second part takes you through the process of establishing an account management system within your firm – setting up the teams, selecting account management staff, assessing client satisfaction, conducting initial meetings, preparing account management plans, cross-selling and interacting with the client on a day-to-day basis.

Part one – The business rationale

What is account management?

There are various ways in which we can view the way in which we provide service to all clients and how this might differ for different types of clients:

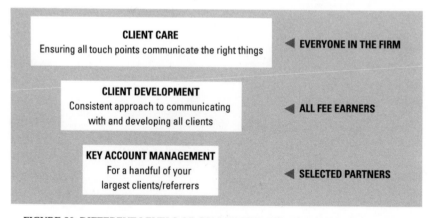

CLIENT CARE
Ensuring all touch points communicate the right things
◀ EVERYONE IN THE FIRM

CLIENT DEVELOPMENT
Consistent approach to communicating with and developing all clients
◀ ALL FEE EARNERS

KEY ACCOUNT MANAGEMENT
For a handful of your largest clients/referrers
◀ SELECTED PARTNERS

FIGURE 20: DIFFERENT LEVELS OF CRM (CLIENT RELATIONSHIP MANAGEMENT)

In essence, the account management programme is a way of organising the firm into client facing teams – and providing the necessary systems, training and resources for those teams – in order to provide an integrated and responsive service to all of a client's needs in a mutually beneficial way, thus enabling both the client and the firm to grow and prosper from the relationship. Ideally, the account management programme should link into the firm's overall strategic positioning (branding) and the way it organises groups, to tackle sector or product specific marketing programmes (see Chapter two on marketing). The following figure shows how client management fits into the overall strategy:

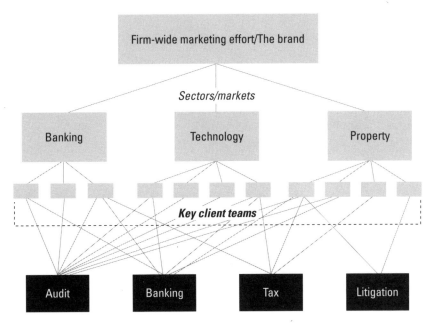

FIGURE 21: LINKING FIRM-WIDE MARKETING
(AND BRANDING) TO MAJOR CLIENT TEAMS
(© KIM TASSO 2000)

Account management can be defined in many ways. Some of the most popular definitions are as follows:

> *Account management is an approach adopted by firms aimed at building a portfolio of loyal key accounts by offering them, on a continuing basis, a service package tailored to their individual needs. To co-ordinate day-to-day interaction under the umbrella of a long-term relationship, firms typically form dedicated teams headed up by a key account manager. This special treatment has significant implications for organising structure, communications and managing expectations.*
>
> **TONY MILLMAN (1995) KEY ACCOUNT MANAGEMENT**

> *I offer the following to the professions:*

> *A client driven series of shared values, procedures and behaviours that, whilst differentiating the firm in a sustainable way yielding a competitive advantage, results in services tailored to specific client needs, high and improving client satisfaction and close and more productive and synergistic relationships with clients which generate an increased level of work referral and greater profits.*

It is important to locate account management within the context of the overall business development process in a professional firm:

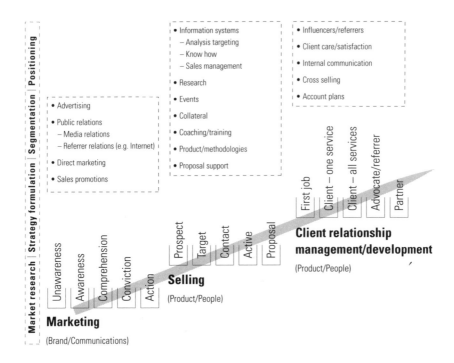

FIGURE 22: THE MARKETING, SELLING AND CLIENT DEVELOPMENT CYCLE
(© KIM TASSO)

Why account management?

Often professionals wonder why a client never gives them anymore work. There can be both general and specific reasons:

GENERAL:

- Advisers have never asked the question.

- Suffers from inertia – the client has not thought about it.

- Loyal to other advisers.

- Lacks knowledge about the services available.

- Lacks knowledge about your firm's capabilities.

- Administrative difficulty, such as transferring files or connecting to a different computer system.

SPECIFIC:

- Perceives you as being too busy to manage their work.

- Perceives that you are not interested in winning more business.

- Has a policy to spread the work and avoid 'too many eggs in one basket'.

- Disorganised and has not addressed new or additional needs.

- Has typecast you as only able to provide one type of service.

- Is being targeted or wooed by one of your competitors.

- Considers individuals (rather than firms) to be most important.

- Selects advisers on a 'horses for courses' basis.

A structured approach to account management can help you unearth the reasons and take positive and appropriate steps to resolve the situation.

Account management brings benefits to both the firm and to the clients. For most firms, a large proportion of annual income comes from a relatively small number of clients. Research shows that:

- It costs several times more to win business from new clients rather than from existing clients.

- Existing clients who are neglected may turn to other advisers.

- Increasing client retention by a small amount can have a significant impact on profitability. (Bain reported it could be as high as a 5% reduction in client loss, leading to a 50% increase in profits.)

- A 10% increase in client loyalty can lead to up to a 20% increase in profits.

- Up to 90% of recommendations are a result of relationship issues.

Clients also benefit from account management:

- A one stop, co-ordinated, integrated and seamless service – clients do not need to concern themselves with the internal structure of the firm.

- A single point of contact – clients have a single point of contact through which all of their requests can be directed.

- Well briefed advisers – all those working on their business are aware of the overall objectives and issues, and are therefore better able to provide their specialist advice and services within the context of an overall framework.

The objectives of account management

The objectives of account management are as follows:

A) TO REALLY KNOW THE CLIENT'S BUSINESS AND NEEDS

To deliver a really good service requires an in-depth understanding of the client's business aims and procedures. Clients rate the ability of their advisers to provide advice in their commercial context very highly. Ensure that all the client's personnel, systems, industry and commercial issues and service requirements are known by the firm and by all those who work with the client – partners, assistants, trainees and secretaries. This enables all members of the client team to:

i) provide a consistently high level of service that is tailored to the client's particular requirements (which in turn will lead to higher client satisfaction); and

ii) identify areas where additional, innovative and added value services can be provided.

B) TO INCREASE THE AMOUNT, RANGE AND QUALITY OF WORK FOR THAT CLIENT

Ensure that a substantial and increasing flow of work over an extended period of time – from a variety of sources within the client – are sent to various parts of the firm. In effect, account management enables the team to 'grow' the client and protect it against approaches from your competitors.

C) TO DIFFERENTIATE YOUR FIRM AND SUPPORT PREMIUM PRICING

Good account management enables you to differentiate the firm from its competitors by providing – consistently and in a way that is not easily copied – a really different experience of team quality and responsiveness (see Chapter two on Marketing). Most clients want an integrated, transparent service with access to all the necessary expertise but with a single (or very few) point of contact as a channel. Clients will pay a premium price for a differentiated service – where the service is perceived as a 'commodity' heavy price competition follows. For the most part, the internal structure of your firm, and its departments, is largely irrelevant to the client and account management ensures that you maintain this outward looking, client focused, cross firm and integrated approach whilst providing the client with a single point of contact.

D) TO CO-ORDINATE ALL THE FIRM'S ACTIVITIES RELATING TO THE CLIENT

To ensure that all activities across the firm, in relation to a particular client, are co-ordinated and viewed from an holistic point of view, whether it is concerned with marketing, business development, entertaining, work processing or billing. The account management team ensures that the firm adopts a co-ordinated and integrated approach to the development of the relationship. This is particularly important where the firm operates from different offices and across international boundaries.

E) TO IMPROVE THE CLIENT'S OVERALL SATISFACTION WITH THE SERVICE

Research shows that satisfaction relates closely to profitability – the more satisfied the client, the more profitable that client will be.

F) TO RETAIN AND DEVELOP THE CLIENT'S RELATIONSHIP

By constantly looking for ways to improve the client relationship, you will protect it from the attempts of competitors to penetrate the client.

There is a useful way to summarise this process (Key account managers pocketbook, Roger Jones):

A chieve a measurable increase in business.

D evelop long-term business relationships.

P rofit from opportunities.

S trengthen communication with client.

F ocus efforts to help you and your client grow.

O rganise internal resources.

C reate awareness of your service within the account.

U nderstand the client's business environment.

S olicit interest in your client amongst your senior management.

Another way to look at it as an ongoing process with the client:

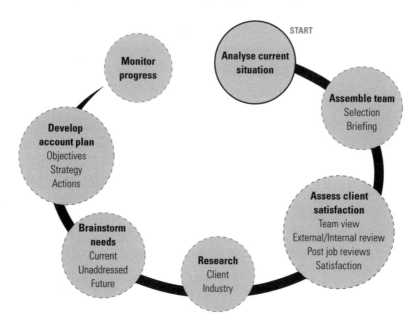

FIGURE 23: THE ACCOUNT MANAGEMENT PROCESS   (© KIM TASSO 2000)

How account management fits into day-to-day life

In some respects, the departmental structure of your firm (if organised along skill or expertise lines) works against the principles of good account management. Therefore, it follows that the account management systems within the firm must form a sort of overlay on your existing structure and procedures. This can make it difficult as professionals may find themselves torn between the demands placed on them by their departments and those placed on them by the best interests of a particular client. The account management systems should provide a mechanism for resolving such conflicts as there will usually be a senior partner whose primary concern will be the well being of the client. If necessary, they can help you manage conflicting departmental and client priorities.

However, the responsibility for account management within a firm is often confused. There should be someone who is responsible for the firm-wide issues, standards and systems of account management (see Chapter nine). However, like all the teams involved in account management there is clearly a need for strong two-way communication to ensure that:

a) the best ideas and practices are shared across the firm; and

b) you adopt and develop your account management procedures in line with changing client needs.

Key elements of the account management process

The overall account management process needs a sustained effort throughout the firm. There are a number of elements requiring different inputs from various people throughout the firm:

- Appoint account partners and managers.
- Develop policies, procedures and systems and document and promote best practice.
- Implement and maintain procedures and systems.
- Provide training and coaching.
- Monitor progress and adherence to standards.
- Assess overall client satisfaction.
- Collect relevant information.
- Establish account teams.
- Supervise internal/external reviews.
- Co-ordinate account plans for sector(s).
- Develop account management plans.
- Oversee implementation of plans.
- Quarterly review of progress – client.
- Quarterly review of progress – firm.
- Manage internal referrals.

It is implicit in account management that the relationship with the client will go through a number of stages (Millman and Wilson, McDonald Millman and Rogers):

DEVELOPMENT STAGE	CHARACTERISTICS
Pre KAM (Key Account Management)	• Relationship distant and transaction focused • Not all relationships potentially key • Both parties assessing the others' potential • Guarded information exchange
Early KAM	• Exploration of possibilities for collaboration • Tentative adaptations to provider's service/process • Providers trying to build social relationships and trust
Mid KAM	• Growth in trust and range of problems addressed • Cross company contact patterns increase • Key account manager takes facilitating rather than lead role • Increasing involvement of senior managers as potential for profitable collaboration increases

Partnership KAM	• Buyer and seller closely aligned • Senior managers from both sides closely involved • Joint teams work on cost saving and quality issues
Synergistic KAM	• Buyer and seller see themselves as a single entity creating joint value in the marketplace
Uncoupling KAM	• Relationship ceases to be strategically important

FIGURE 24: STAGES OF KEY ACCOUNT MANAGEMENT (KAM)*

*Footnote: Reprinted by permission of Butterworth Heinemann Publishers, a division of Reed Education and Professional Publishing Ltd. *CIM Handbook*.

Part two – Taking action

Where do you start?

This section is designed to provide assistance to individual account partners and account managers. The first task is to establish an account team and to arrange for the team to have a preliminary meeting to discuss ideas and a way forward.

Once an account team has been established, the next action is to establish the current level of client satisfaction with the firm's service. This can be done in a number of ways: through self-analysis, external or internal service reviews, senior partner calls or the firm's overall client satisfaction surveys.

Once these preliminary steps have been completed, the account manager should co-ordinate the production of an account plan which:

- Draws together all of the information within the firm about the client.

- Promotes discussion and ideas by the account team.

- Identifies gaps in the firm's knowledge about the client (and how to fill them).

- Sets out procedures and guidance on how the client will be served.

- Provides a clear plan of action for the future.

- Communicates with all those working for that client.

- Measures the progress made with the client over time.

The full account management plan (see Appendix five) provides a method of collecting and organising all the relevant information and planning the future development of the account. A summary version (see Appendix six) is available for those with limited time or resources, although you are encouraged to attempt the full plan approach as the process of analysing and planning generally results in better quality plans. As with marketing planning, the journey is more important than the destination.

Like all good marketing and selling, the account planning process should concentrate first on the client's needs and then on how the firm can provide future services to meet these needs.

Establishing the account team

The account team will probably comprise of a number of professionals with specific responsibilities in account management (note that the specific terms used may vary in your firm). For example:

- **Client/contact partner**: Overall responsibility for supervising client work on a day-to-day basis.

- **Account partner**: Overall responsibility for account management and client care.

- **Account manager**: Supporting role to account partner in the development and implementation of the account management plan.

- **Market specialists**: Those with particular knowledge of the client's market.

- **Skill specialists**: Those with particular skills or expertise that are important to the client's needs.

- **Knowledge managers**: Whose task is to ensure all information about the client and its market are kept appropriately within the firm's systems.

Role of the account partner

The day-to-day work for each client will be managed and supervised by a contact or matter partner. However, the account partner (who may or may not have day-to-day responsibility for the client's work) will be responsible for the following:

- The production of an account plan.

- The achievement of targets identified in the account plan.

- Ensuring that all members of the team are aware of the client's preferences and operating procedures.

- Providing background information about the client's business and industry. This will also include ensuring that all staff working for the client have the relevant skills and knowledge.

- Developing and maintaining relations at the highest level with the client.

- Directing opportunities which arise in the account to the relevant partner in the firm.

- Maintaining overall control of the budgets and income from the client.

- Ensuring that all work is carried out to the highest standards.

- Reading a wide variety of the client's industry press to remain alert to changes in the client's industry and business, ensuring all members of the team are aware of such changes and the impact they may have on future work or work practices.

- Organising and undertaking an internal service review (audit) at least once a year, communicating the results to the rest of the team and ensuring that action is taken to tackle any issues identified by the client.

- Looking for opportunities in the rest of the firm's client and contact base to introduce the client to relevant networking contacts and/ or business opportunities.

- Co-ordinating any efforts to pitch for new or additional work with the client.

- Ensuring that any publicity for the firm is cleared with the client.
- Providing a first point of contact to the client in case of any problems, concerns or complaints that may arise and providing a swift response.

Role of the account manager

- First point of contact for the client on a day-to-day basis – all client enquiries, receiving, interpreting and allocating instructions.
- Understand the client's business.
- Co-ordinate all instructions and delivery of services.
- Progress reporting in the agreed manner with the client.
- The production and maintenance of an account plan – chasing team members to complete actions they have agreed to.
- Preparation of a directory of staff and services in the firm of specific interest to the client. (In more technologically advanced firms this directory may be in the form of a tailored extranet where clients can easily access information about the firm's personnel, services and expertise in a format tailored to their particular organisation and needs.)
- Scheduling and organising regular internal meetings of the account team as well as less formal team communications.
- Maintenance of all information about the client and the account team.
- Regular internal communication about the client, both within and beyond the account team.
- Ensuring that the information held about the client in the firm's databases and other internal systems is accurate and comprehensive. (E.g. that the appropriate contacts are on the appropriate mailing lists, ensuring that the relevant people are invited to the firm's social and business events, that the client's staff have the relevant access to the extranets etc.)

- Appoint and brief specialists to carry out specific functions or activities for the client.
- Meeting with the client regularly to review progress, plan future work and provide overall advice and direction.
- Act as a conduit through which all the key developments of the firm are communicated, where relevant, to the appropriate contacts at the client organisation.

Qualities and attributes of account partners and managers

Account management staff need to be well versed in many skills and exhibit many attributes and qualities in order to be successful in their role:

Personal qualities

- Integrity.
- Adaptable (professionally and personally) and responsive to client needs.
- Resilient/persistent.
- Selling/negotiating skills.
- 'Likeability'.
- Keen and enthusiastic and prepared to think like the client so that they can be proactive in identifying opportunities.

Subject knowledge

- Specific professional service expertise/knowledge.
- Understanding of the business environment and markets of clients.
- Financial/budgetary knowledge.
- Legal/compliance knowledge.
- Computer literacy.

Firm knowledge

- Understanding of the breadth of the firm's knowledge base.
- Experience of all the firm's systems and capabilities.
- Familiarity with all the firm's services and expertise.
- 'Helicopter view' of the entire client base.

Thinking skills

- Empathy/understanding the client's point of view.
- Creativity and flexibility.
- Strategic planning and thinking.
- 'Boundary spanning' – thinking outside the box.

Managerial skills

- Focused on the end results of any professional advice – efficiency, effectiveness and profitability.
- Communication – including listening and persuading.
- People management and leadership.
- Credibility – boardroom to postroom.
- Administrative/organisation.

Client and professional skills

- Understand the client's business, aims, plans and market dynamics.
- Ability to have an overview of the client's entire range of professional needs and how they interact.

Assembling the account team

The first action for the account partner and account manager is to assemble the relevant account team. The following issues should be considered:

- Who has worked on the client's business in the past?
- Who works on the client's business at present?
- Who does the client like and have a good bond with?
- Who else in the firm should be part of the team?
- Which people can provide services to the client that are not currently used?

It may be that there is a core account management team, which undertakes the majority of the work, and a broader 'circulation' list of other people in the firm who need to be kept aware of developments with that client.

The first meeting

The account partner should then arrange a first internal meeting of the account management team.

The purpose of the first meeting is to:

- Ensure that everyone in the account team is at a basic level of understanding about the client's business and relationship with the firm.
- Help the team bond by focusing on areas for improvement.
- Identify a clear action path for the future.
- Initiate the preparation of an account management plan.

An example agenda for the first meeting is as follows:

1 Brief history of the client relationship (length, source of introduction etc.).

2 Overview of the client's industry and business.

3   Summary of the key individuals at the client organisation.

4   Summary of the main jobs completed and fees generated.

5   Gaps in knowledge where the firm needs to undertake research.

6   Aims for the future.

7   Discussion of the results of the team members questionnaire on self-appraisal (see Appendix three).

8   Problem areas and necessary action.

9   Next steps.

At the end of the meeting, the account manager should prepare detailed minutes of the meeting and start to prepare an account management plan (see Appendix five).

Assessing the client's satisfaction

The starting point for the development of an account management plan is an objective review of the quality of service provided to a particular client. Such a review will help identify where the relationship needs to be strengthened, where the quality of service needs to be improved and where there are opportunities for developing further business.

There are a number of ways in which the service provided is assessed:

Coach

You could ask your coach or 'mentor' within the client organisation (see the decision-making unit in Chapter five) to provide you with some feedback. You must take care here as, by definition, this individual is likely to have a positive view of you and your firm's performance. However, often your friends within the client organisation will feel more comfortable giving you honest feedback and constructive criticism, and will do so because they want to see you improve your performance and standing within the client organisation.

Self-appraisal

The questions in the self appraisal form (see Appendix three) are designed to promote discussion amongst the team about their perceptions of their performance in delivering a high quality service to the client. From research it is known that those attributes listed are highly valued by clients. Complete the questionnaire individually and then discuss them as a team to identify where views of client service may differ.

External service reviews

It is good practice for your firm to arrange for an independent consultant to interview the firm's key clients through an in-depth and structured face-to-face interview (see Chapter nine – Firm-wide issues).

Typically, the consultant will interview at least two but up to four individuals at the nominated client organisation. The consultant should send a detailed report of the interviews to the relevant client and account partners. Once the nominated major clients have been interviewed, there is typically an overall report summarising the main findings, trends and conclusions which is distributed and/or communicated more widely within the firm. The overall report is a good source of information for all account teams as it summarises some of the issues uncovered with a number of clients that are likely to apply to many other client situations.

Once the account partner has read the report, he or she will take a number of actions:

a)   Meet with the researcher to discuss the issues raised more fully and to develop an action plan of the most pressing actions necessary.

b)   Meet with the rest of the account team to discuss both the positive and negative aspects of the feedback and agree how to tackle the immediate changes needed.

c)   Arrange to visit the client to discuss the points raised in more detail.

d)   Produce an account management plan.

Internal service reviews

Where an external review is considered inappropriate, or to continue the process with a client where there has been an external service review, the account partner is responsible for ensuring that at least once a year they undertake an internal service review with the client.

The purpose of the service review is to obtain as much information as possible from the client about the nature of the relationship and the past work, to see how their satisfaction can be enhanced (thus strengthening the relationship) and to identify any additional areas of opportunity. An example questionnaire and guidance is shown in Appendix four.

Before the service review meeting

At an appropriate time, the account partner will mention to the client that an opportunity to discuss the firm's work and the client's satisfaction in a formal way would be appreciated. A date for some time in the future will be set with perhaps one or two of the client's senior directors. A short confirmatory letter will be sent shortly after the arrangements have been made and this will highlight the key areas to be discussed, namely:

- The performance of the firm over the past 12-18 months.
- Where the firm has performed well.
- Where the firm could improve its service.
- Any areas the client would like to discuss in particular.

The account partner will then contact all those within the firm who have been involved with the client and will collect information about what has been conducted well, where issues arose and areas on which the client is likely to comment. Ideally, the account partner should have a series of specific questions – in addition to those in the questionnaire – which he or she hopes to address with the client.

At the service review meeting

At the service review meeting, the account partner will use a questionnaire (see example in Appendix four) to provide some structure to the discussion but will follow the lead of the client in pursuing issues that they raise. In effect, the questionnaire is there as a tool and not as an end in itself.

Start talking about the broad relationship and satisfaction issues before delving into specifics. By asking broad questions at the outset, the client will be viewing the relationship as a whole rather than concentrating on the matters specifically happening at present.

Keep the meeting to a specific time frame – no more than 45 minutes.

Ensure that if/when the client raises problems or issues, the partner simply listens and takes notes. Aim to spend less than 30% of the time speaking. Use probing, open questions (who, why, what, where etc. – see the material on questioning in Chapter six) and silences to encourage the client to speak. Ask for examples of good and bad experiences. Once a question is posed, allow the client time to think about their answer – this may require you to adopt a period of silence for a short while.

A defensive attitude should not be adopted as the client will cease to reveal his or her concerns. Although opportunities to sell may arise during the meeting, the temptation should be resisted. A further meeting can be arranged for this. It is important that the original aim of the meeting – to listen and to gather information – is maintained. Furthermore, the partner should not attempt to explain or make excuses for any action with which the client is dissatisfied.

Do not be embarrassed if the client starts to talk about personality clashes or other difficult subjects. Simply listen and take notes. Ask what his or her colleagues think – it is often easier to convey unpleasant or difficult messages when doing so on behalf of someone else, rather than one's own feelings and perceptions.

If it does get tough, either ask the client what they would have preferred to happen or, in a really tight spot, be prepared to offer some alternatives yourself.

At all times, observe the body language (non-verbal communication – see Chapter six) of the client to see if they are holding back, feeling defensive or feeling uncomfortable. Ensure that your own body language conveys confidence and interest.

At the end of the meeting, thank the client for his/her time. Summarise the key points that arose and offer the client the chance to add any further points or clarify anything. Explain what will happen next.

After the meeting

After the meeting, the account partner should undertake a number of actions:

- Write to the client to thank them for their time. Indicate that any issues raised are being addressed and that a further communication will deal with this in more detail and provide a time scale.

- Write up the detailed notes from the meeting and circulate them to the relevant members of the account team and any firm-wide system where overall trends are analysed.

- Arrange for the account team to get together – along with anyone else necessary in the firm – to discuss what action will be taken as a result of the review. An action plan should be produced and/or the account management plan for the client updated.

- A follow-up session with the client (either a letter explaining the planned changes or a further meeting) should be arranged.

- Progress should be reviewed on a quarterly basis.

Senior partner calls

Another simple but effective system in a firm is where the senior partner of the firm has a system which prompts him or her to contact, each week, one or two of the firm's major clients to ask them about their satisfaction with the service provided. The senior partner will, of course, contact the account partner in advance of making the call to obtain any highlights or a briefing on any issues before making the call.

In addition to providing an additional channel of communication to the client (there may be instances where the client is unwilling to reveal some information to his or her account partner or account manager) the call will demonstrate to the client that their business is valued by the firm.

Client satisfaction surveys

Many firms operate a central system whereby the views of a large number of clients are gathered on a regular basis (see Chapter nine on Firm-wide issues). Some firms issue these questionnaires with bills and others with key firm mailings. The process is useful to account partners in the following ways:

a) **General information**: It provides general information about how clients perceive the service and highlights common areas of concern that may be relevant to your client.

b) **Benchmark**: It enables you to benchmark the satisfaction of your client against the satisfaction of the firm's major clients generally.

c) **Specific information**: If your client is included in the survey, you may be able to obtain a copy of their completed questionnaire which will enable you to explore the issues identified in more depth – perhaps through a more detailed internal client service review (see above).

d) **Measuring improvement**: Where your client participates regularly in the survey you will have a direct measure of how the client team has improved in its service provision.

e) **Input for account management plan**: The specific information about your client can be used to direct activity and plan action in your account management plan.

Relationship management

Relationship management is a wide and complex subject drawing on a vast range of techniques and research from marketing, selling and account management literature and training materials. It would be impossible to provide a comprehensive review of all the subject matter that might be relevant to account partners and management but some of the most useful models and guidance are shown below:

Evolution of the client relationship

Like the earlier figure showing the stages of KAM (Key Account Management) it may help to view the client relationship as an evolutionary process:

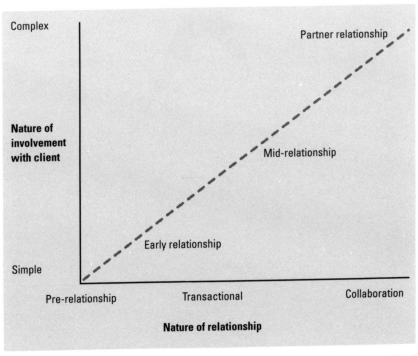

FIGURE 25: EVOLUTION OF CLIENT RELATIONSHIPS (MILLMAN & WILSON, 1994)

Mapping the relationship

An early and helpful activity is to map out all of the contacts at a client organisation, including those you know and those you don't know:

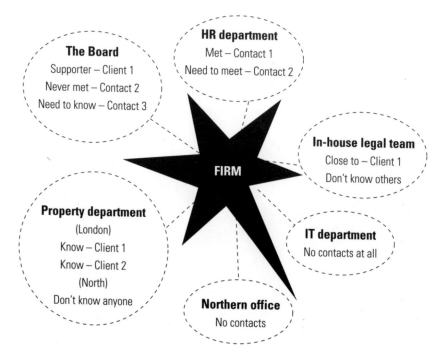

FIGURE 26: A MAP OF CONTRACTS (© KIM TASSO)

Once you have completed the initial map, there are a number of analyses you can undertake to gain a deeper understanding of the roles of individuals and possible actions you might take. For example:

You can use a simple classification system (e.g. Traffic lights, red for concern, amber for unknown and green for good) to sort out which of the individuals at the client organisation are supporters of your firm. Some firms adopt a 'friend or foe' classification system.

You then need to develop some 'shift' strategies to move contacts in the right relationship direction.

The map will also help identify the members of the decision-making unit (see Chapter four) at the client organisation.

These two analyses may well reveal some political issues within the client organisation that must be known by all members of the account team.

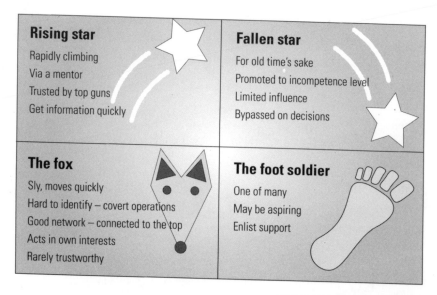

FIGURE 28: CLIENT POLITICS*

Matching people and personalities

Inevitably, the individuals at the client organisation will have a preference for dealing with people at your firm with whom they share the same background and personalities (see Chapter four on Buyer behaviour). This means that on occasions there may be situations where there is a mismatch and a lack of personal rapport or chemistry gets in the way of the relationship being developed.

A mature and pragmatic approach is needed when such situations occur and no one at your firm should feel uncomfortable or awkward about flagging up such situations and/or being prepared to shift responsibilities to someone else with whom the client is more likely to get on.

Account partners and managers who know their clients well will be much better placed to anticipate where personality clashes are likely to arise and therefore take action to prevent them occurring.

*Footnote: With permission of Roger Jones and Management Pocketbooks

Systems

There will be a number of systems within your firm where you will be required to enter and maintain information about your major accounts (see Chapter nine on Firm-wide issues). This might include mailing information (e.g. marketing databases), entertainment programmes, contact management systems, client files, quality systems, internal knowledge bases, jobs lists, work in progress, firm-wide presentations, extranets and intranets, sector plans, account plans and forecasting systems.

Your firm may also operate a client care or quality programme which you will need to implement with your major accounts. Your firm may have documented its policy or best practice which you need to learn and apply to your major accounts.

You can increase client loyalty by providing them with additional access (usually through the web or an extranet) to your internal computer systems – whether this is the work in progress, project management or knowledge base of the firm. This area is developing very rapidly in the professions at present, with e-business providing some innovative ways to enhance service delivery and to create closer partnerships with clients.

Day-to-day communication

Each client, and each individual at that client, will have different preferences for their day-to-day communications. For example, some clients will want to be kept informed of every step of the process and others will only want to know when the task is complete. Some clients will prefer communications by email and voicemail and others will abhor these methods and prefer face-to-face meetings and letters.

It is the task of the account partner and account manager to know and communicate these preferences, and for everyone in the account team to modify their preferred working practices to reflect those of the client.

Some firms prepare tailored guides, directories or extranets for major clients to facilitate better communication and to demonstrate that the range of relevant expertise is available.

Planned activities

Your account plan should contain a series of actions for the following 12 months that ensure your objectives for the account are achieved. Such activities might include entertaining, mailshots, joint activities or internal service reviews. You may need access to marketing expertise if you are to organise effective marketing (e.g. seminars) or entertaining events (e.g. attendance at sponsored sports or arts events) or mailings (see Chapter two on Marketing).

You might also invite members of the client to attend internal training courses or seminars – so that they can share in your continuing professional development (CPD) programmes and meet a wider range of people at your firm.

You might decide to second a member of your team to the client at a preferential rate, in order to develop a deeper knowledge of their business and build a wider network of contacts within the organisation.

A regular review of your progress against the plan will help keep everyone focused on what must be done to strengthen the relationship and win more business from the client.

Proactive

Clients often ask their advisors to be more proactive. This means calling them up or writing to them with ideas to improve their business. An excellent example is in an international property firm where the account partner attempted to develop a '60 ideas in 60 minutes' list for his client to show how much he was thinking about the client's business. The client was very impressed and grateful – and several ideas were adopted.

NINE
Firm-wide issues on selling

ROADMAP

This chapter is designed for those with responsibility for managing firms who have to ensure that the appropriate attitudes and systems exist to allow selling to flourish. Issues covered include: managing change, culture, business and marketing strategy, role models, time and recognition, feast and famine, ethics and professionalism, involvement of junior staff, motivation, loyalty to individuals, appraisals, research, training, coaching, incentives, systems and priorities.

As a senior partner or director with responsibility for management you will inevitably be faced with a number of firm-wide decisions relating to selling. Even the most gifted professional will have difficulty selling in a firm where the culture and systems are 'anti-selling'. This chapter aims to highlight some of the issues that may exist in your firm and provide some guidance on how they might be addressed.

Managing change

There are a variety of changes that may be needed to enhance selling within a firm – sometimes these are relatively small changes but often they are major changes which require fundamental shifts in attitude and behaviour. The management of change is a huge subject in its own right. I have only space here to flag up that it is a vitally important issue and to illustrate the overall process of change (affecting both organisations and individuals) so you can learn more about it before embarking on a change programme.

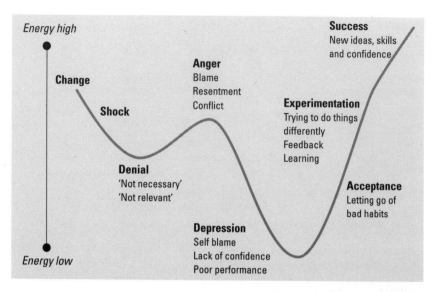

FIGURE 29: THE CHANGE CYCLE

Another key tool to help you understand the drivers and inhibitors of change is the force field analysis. An example is shown below:

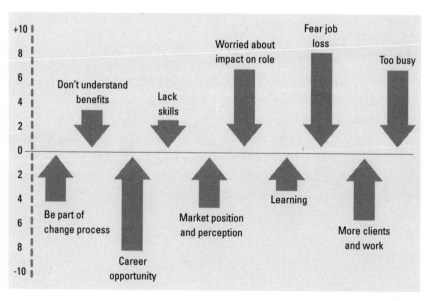

FIGURE 30: THE CHANGE CYCLE FORCE FIELD ANALYSIS

Culture

One of the biggest factors contributing to the success of selling at a professional practice is the prevailing culture (the firm's 'personality' expressed as 'the way we do things around here'). Some firms have a culture that is aggressive and focused on winning new business. Some firms have a culture where overt marketing and selling behaviour is frowned upon. Some firms give kudos to the new business wins and undervalue the retention and development of existing clients.

Most professional firms have a culture that is risk averse and where failure is fatal. Professionals in these environments shy away from selling because they fear that a sales failure (and there are always inevitably some) will result in a career failure. In these situations, senior management must show that failure is acceptable (providing it is within the context of a carefully thought through plan and due to factors beyond the control of the individual).

The first step is to understand the culture of your firm and identify ways to modify it in the way required but without losing the very essence of your practice. Changing the culture of your practice is a difficult task and one that is unlikely to happen quickly. However, there are a number of things you can do to facilitate the process, here are some examples:

- Arrange a series of awareness raising sessions where an outside facilitator or a member of another, non-competing firm, comes along to talk about issues such as marketing and selling and how they have been useful in other firms. Get those at the session to offer their ideas and thoughts. Build a modest programme of activities around the ideas and ensure they are carried out over the next few months.

- Ask partners to spend some time considering which aspects of the firm's culture support the firm's strengths and weaknesses (this may be through a questionnaire or at a workshop at a partners' retreat) and then compile and discuss the issues. Getting everyone's agreement that certain behaviours and attitudes need to be modified is a first step on the path.

- Provide a structured series of training courses to provide all the key 'influencers' in the firm with the required skills to go out and start practising different marketing and selling behaviours.

Business and marketing strategy

A key inhibitor of successful sales activity in a professional firm is the lack of a framework in terms of what sort of clients and business the firm wants to develop and the roles and responsibility for developing the various areas. Without a clear strategy, fee earners will tend to go off and pursue their own interests and contacts in a haphazard way, which is usually inefficient.

With a clear plan for what the firm is trying to achieve – at a firm-wide level, by different markets, perhaps by department (although as a marketer I would argue that your segmentation should be based on client groups rather than internal structures!) and by partner group – each member of the firm will see how they can best contribute. Good plans – that analyse the current position, set goals and outline the strategies being pursued to achieve those goals – will help pull the firm in the same direction. There is some guidance on producing marketing plans in Chapter two.

The plans should also identify the major existing clients that need development (see Chapter eight on Account management) and management as well as target new clients the firm is trying to win. Articulating the client and target lists will also ensure that you do not have several members of the firm all targeting the same client/target in an uncoordinated and potentially embarrassing way. A clear plan – with measurable objectives – will also enable everyone to see what progress is being made which has a motivating effect.

Involvement of junior staff

In many firms, marketing and selling are the preserve of the partners. In more forward thinking firms, they involve professionals in the marketing and selling process from the outset of their professional careers. In addition to broadening the number of people promoting your firm to existing and prospective clients, it also means that younger staff develop the required skills at a much earlier stage of their careers. This increases their value to the firm and reduces the shock and impact when they become partners and are suddenly expected to generate business for the first time.

However, you will need clear guidelines in terms of what younger staff should and should not be doing. Their first priority is obviously to develop their professional skills and do a good job for existing clients. Explain how they can act as ambassadors and the 'eyes and ears' of the firm with existing clients – remaining alert to concerns or opportunities to cross sell. Provide them with enough information about the services and clients of the firm so that they can speak confidently when talking in social contexts. Offer some basic training where they can ask questions and offer ideas. Allow them to access the firm's senior partners so that they can observe 'selling skills in action'. Provide them with business cards that they can distribute amongst their peers.

Some firms even establish business development groups for trainees who then forge close relationships (through informal presentations, joint training sessions and sports and social events) with their peers in related potentially referring organisations – thus 'growing their own' network of contacts for the future.

Where marketing, business development, sales or account management plans exist – arrange internal meetings and briefings where they can be explained to and discussed by more junior staff. In addition to helping them understand the overall aims it will help them identify areas and tasks where they can offer support (e.g. in undertaking research, in organising events, in developing their knowledge of the clients and markets) and spread the load shouldered by the partners.

Time and recognition

A constant concern of professionals is that they lack the necessary time to devote to marketing and selling and, similarly, when they do devote time it is not valued or recognised by the firm. You must ensure that you are not giving conflicting messages (e.g. asking fee-earners to devote time to marketing and client development but then only rewarding chargeable time).

If your reward (and appraisal) systems operate solely on the basis of total chargeable hours then partners and staff will be reluctant to devote time to marketing and selling. Therefore, you may have to consider reducing your chargeable hour targets for some or all of your professional staff. However, it is important that the time they spend in business development activities is captured and monitored. Too many firms do not encourage professionals to record 'non-chargeable' time but it is one of the firm's most expensive assets and should be managed accordingly. A simple series of time sheet codes (if you get too elaborate the professionals will fail to use them) that separates out:

- marketing (e.g. seminars, articles, conferences etc.);
- selling (e.g. pitches, meetings with potential clients); and
- account management (e.g. entertaining existing clients, developing account plans etc.).

An alternative method is to set up separate codes for major marketing, client development projects or pitches so that you can assess your opportunity costs and cost-of-sales on a firm-wide basis as well as monitor (and reward) the contribution of individuals.

This should enable you to assess the level (and results of) business development activity for individuals and particular teams.

Role models

Regardless of the formal procedures and policies that exist within your firm, professionals will tend to follow the behaviour of those people in the firm who are regarded as the most senior and/or successful. Typically, younger professionals will model their behaviour and attitudes on their departmental heads in the hope that this is the appropriate way to further their careers.

Therefore, before implementing changes to increase successful selling activities, consider which senior members of the firm are most respected and followed by their peers and juniors, and focus initial efforts on getting them to change.

Needless to say, any initiative or idea that meets with these role models' disapproval or criticism is unlikely to succeed so you must ensure they are on-board before rolling out your programmes more widely.

Some firms have identified business development or client management 'champions' across different parts of the organisation – thus providing role models other than the departmental heads. The success of this approach depends on the relative political power and status these individuals have within the firm.

Feast and famine

The classic situation in a professional firm is that everyone is seriously over busy and then everyone is worried because there is no work. The natural reaction is to ignore business development activities whilst the firm is busy and to get everyone involved in the process when things are quiet. This perpetuates the feast-famine cycle.

Your marketing strategy (see Chapter two) should address the current and desired balance of transactional versus ongoing work and also the balance between cyclical and anti-cyclical types of client and work. This in itself should help even the peaks and troughs.

You should also ensure that your marketing plans have activities that can be undertaken during busy times that are not designed to generate more work immediately but to have some benefit in the medium to long-term. For example, profile building activities will position the firm well for the future, without necessarily creating demand for work today. Initiating contact with 'cold' prospects is unlikely to yield immediate work in view of the length of the selling cycle (see Chapter five).

Similarly, when times are quiet, the marketing plan should contain additional projects and activities that can be implemented relatively quickly to have an immediate impact on new instructions.

However, only those firms that maintain a constant and consistent approach to business development are likely to overcome the feast-famine cycle entirely.

Ethics and professionalism

Every profession has professional rules and most of them address the appropriate behaviours in marketing and selling. For example, some professional rules still forbid some types of cold calling and restrict fee-sharing arrangements with third parties. There is also general legislation – such as the Data Protection Act – that can impact on selling activity. Someone within the firm must take responsibility for being aware of the rules and ensuring compliance. Some firms take the view that some of the professional rules are not in the interests of the clients and have their own policies and procedures. Whether you decide to abide by the rules or not, and whether you wish to interpret them to the letter or in spirit, knowing what the rules are – and making contact with the ethics personnel at your professional association – is a must.

Loyalty to individuals versus loyalty to the firm

The downside of having professional staff who are effective at selling is that the clients tend to be loyal to the individual rather than to the firm. This means that when the member of staff moves on, the client goes with them. There are measures that the firm can take to guard against (but not prevent) this from occurring. For example, you could implement a policy that at least two senior people must have a relationship with the client. Alternatively, that within six months of first instructions, a senior partner from another department must be introduced to the client or assign a 'relationship manager' role as well as a 'day-to-day work co-ordination' manager. Chapter eight on Account management addresses these issues.

Appraisals

Your appraisal system will be important for sales success in at least two ways. First, the appraisal system will help you to identify the training needs in your firm – which areas of the marketing and business development process cause concern, which specific skills the professionals would like to develop etc. Second, it will enable you to filter down the firm's, department's and office's overall marketing and selling targets to specific individuals. Once a professional knows that part of their performance assessment will depend on their sales success, they will devote more time and energy to these areas.

If your firm uses a form for appraisals, where appraisers and appraisees complete questions in advance of an appraisal meeting, the sort of section you should consider adding might look as follows:

Skill and activity	Appraisee's/ Appraiser's comments	Development needs	Objectives for year	Grade
Marketing: Strategic Development of marketing plan for market, segment or area of expertise. Development and supervision of a team with marketing targets.				
Marketing: Tactical Profile raising (e.g. speeches, articles, seminars), research and materials development. Intermediary liaison.				

Skill and activity	Appraisee's/ Appraiser's comments	Development needs	Objectives for year	Grade
Selling: New business Establishing contact with new targets, entertaining, meetings, proposals, presentations and pitches.				
Selling: Existing clients Developing account plans, assessing satisfaction, cross selling.				
Other business development All other activities e.g. systems development, training of others, analysis etc.				

FIGURE 31: AN APPRAISAL FORM (© KIM TASSO)

Research

There are a number of research programmes that can support and enhance selling and account management activities. In Chapter eight on Account management, a number of firm-wide systems are mentioned including:

Client satisfaction

A regular measure of the satisfaction amongst the firm's major clients against a series of key elements of the service (e.g. responsiveness, accuracy, quality etc.). This provides quantitative information about the firm's performance and a benchmark against which progress across the firm and within specific clients can be measured. The use of rating scales (e.g. 1 for poor and 5 for excellent) is common.

Service reviews

Some firms commission the services of external researchers to undertake in-depth face-to-face or telephone interviews with major clients to obtain more qualitative information about how clients perceive the firm and their satisfaction. Organising these programmes centrally adds an element of objectivity which can be lacking if left to the various account teams.

POST TENDER REVIEWS

In Chapter seven on Competitive tendering, the need for post tender reviews is mentioned. These are very similar to service reviews except that they often take place with organisations which are not clients, as your firm has failed to win their work at a competitive tender.

KNOWLEDGE MANAGERS AND RESEARCHERS

As well as staff allocated to collect and manage technical and professional information (e.g precedents or cases in legal environments, standards in accounting markets, rental information and economic indicators in the property sector) you should have personnel or external resources available to undertake research into particular client markets or of specific organisations to support marketing plans, sales strategies and competitive tenders.

Training

As most professionals do not receive training in marketing, selling and client care as part of their professional training it is important to provide ways of acquiring the relevant knowledge and skills. Although there are commercial training providers who offer public courses in these subjects, typically they are not well received by professionals as often they do not use examples and case studies that relate to their professional services.

There are, however, specialist training and conference providers – usually well-known within each profession – that do provide the relevant courses. However, this can be an expensive way to provide training to everyone in the firm so it may be necessary to select a few individuals to receive this sort of training and make other arrangements for remaining staff. Alternatively, you can ask these providers to produce in-house courses for you that are tailored to the needs and issues within your firm but using tried and tested sales techniques, from other parts of the commercial world.

It is also important to remember that selling covers a wide variety of skills and topics (see Chapter six) so any training programme you produce internally or with the aid of external advisers should be modular – allowing professionals to hone those skills where they are weakest. The list of books in Appendix two may give some clues to the different skill areas that may appeal. There are also videos and other training support materials available from commercial educational providers, who specialise in the professions. It may be necessary to provide some general awareness raising workshops to help professionals identify those areas where they are particularly keen to receive training.

There are other ways to increase the level of selling skills within your firm. You can identify those senior professionals who have a good track record and exemplary selling skills. You can then allocate younger members of staff to accompany these people at meetings or networking events (this is sometimes referred to as 'shadowing'), so that they can observe the behaviours first hand. Alternatively, these exemplars can be asked to work with professional trainers or facilitators who can extract their techniques, ideas and anecdotes so that they can be built into your own training programme. Similarly, at regular departmental meetings you can ask different professionals to present a short analysis of a sale which describes the process they went through to win the business from a particular client.

As with any training, it is important that the firm has clear objectives before it begins and that it measures the success of the training – perhaps in terms of increased business from new and existing clients – at an appropriate point after the training. The firm should also accept that training on its own is unlikely to provide a solution and that it can take time for selling competencies to be developed.

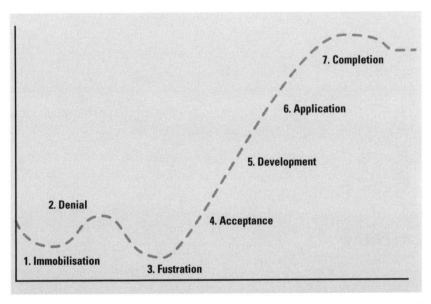

FIGURE 32: THE COMPETENCE CURVE

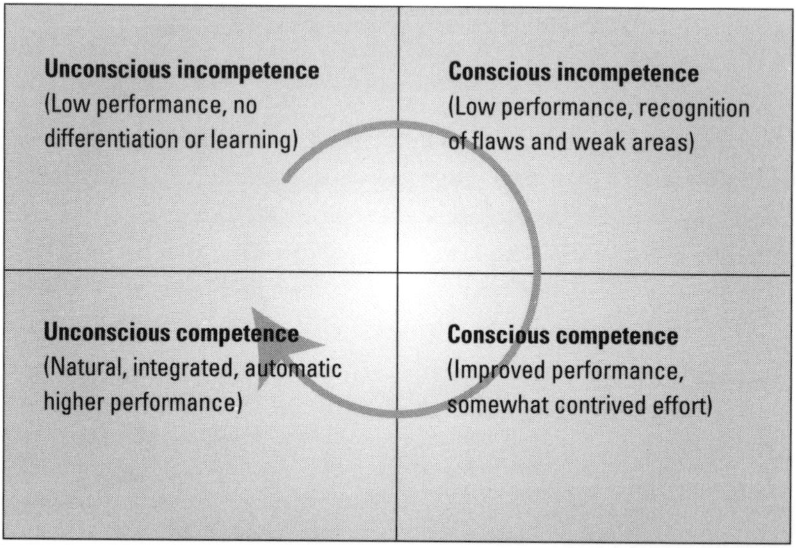

Unconscious incompetence (Low performance, no differentiation or learning)	Conscious incompetence (Low performance, recognition of flaws and weak areas)
Unconscious competence (Natural, integrated, automatic higher performance)	Conscious competence (Improved performance, somewhat contrived effort)

FIGURE 33: THE LEARNING PROCESS

Coaching

Increasingly, firms are recognising the limitations of the traditional forms of training and are making greater use of coaches and mentors to improve short-term performance. Providing you have professional qualified coaches who are familiar with the specific issues faced by the professions this can be a highly effective way to improve sales performance.

Recent examples of how coaching can work is following a general training course on the principles of marketing and selling, the coach worked with six fee-earners on a one-to-one basis to a) develop their own personal business development plans and b) implement those plans over a period of nine months.

As well as using external coaches, you can provide training to existing partners and senior staff so that they can act as coaches to younger members of the firm.

Incentives

The issue of financial incentives for new business generated or cross referrals is a controversial one. Most professional firms argue that it is everyone's duty to develop new business and therefore refuse to pay any special financial incentives to those who do. Other firms feel that the generation of new business, or effective cross-selling, should be rewarded financially and have complex systems for ensuring that introducing partners receive a percentage of new income for a specific time.

Whatever policy exists in your firm should be examined carefully to see whether it is producing the desired results. There may be a case for introducing a scheme for a limited time in order to help new practices and behaviours become established. There may be a case for developing a scheme that incentivises entire departments or teams – for new business or referrals or both. Some firms operate a 'super profit' scheme where all professional staff can benefit from new business generated beyond what is planned for the year.

Systems to support selling

There are a number of different systems (some computer based) that you will need to implement to achieve maximum sales effectiveness at your firm. Some of the key systems are mentioned below:

Marketing or CRM database

There should be a central system which contains all the information about existing clients, referrers and prospective clients. As well as providing a central source of information about existing clients (e.g. to do conflict checks, to co-ordinate invitations to events and mailings etc.) the database – if linked to fee information – will also support both marketing analyses (e.g. segmentation, response rates, profitability etc. – see Chapter two) that can assist in targeting and account management programmes (see Chapter eight). You will need a policy on the inclusion of 'cold' contact information, such as that available on a purchased mailing list and 'warm' information generated as a result of enquiries to marketing programmes.

Referral management

Some firms have systems that analyse the amount of work being generated by a particular client for different service or market teams within the firm. These cross-selling systems are sometimes linked to incentive schemes to ensure that existing clients are developed. Sometimes these systems are designed to ensure that the overall account manager is kept aware – at all times and usually by automatic email – of the flow of instructions from the client, regardless to which part of the firm.

A simple system is illustrated below:

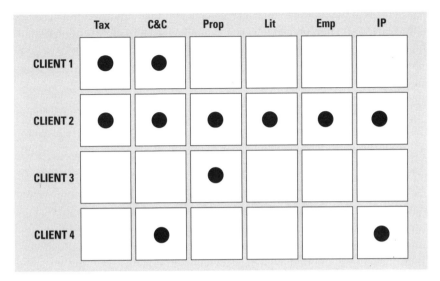

FIGURE 34: SIMPLE CROSS-SELLING MATRIX – TO MONITOR INTERNAL REFERRALS

Intermediary management

In some firms, a significant amount of marketing and sales effort is directed not at the end clients but at organisations who might refer work, such as other professionals, banks and venture capitalists etc. These systems might be oriented towards contact management or towards measuring the flow of referrals and some sort of reciprocity system.

Similar systems to the cross-selling matrix above can be deployed to measure intermediary programmes.

Risk management

In addition to a marketing plan and agreed target list, some firms have teams available to assess the attractiveness and risk of potential new clients or assignments. This is valuable when deciding whether or not to submit proposals in response to a tender.

A contact management system

Focusing on a contact management system can help structure and measure sales activities. There is some merit in having a separate contact or sales management system, if fee-earners are spending a significant amount of time selling. These systems can integrate with word processing, email and scheduling software as well as telephones to automate activities such as record view when receiving an incoming phone call, prompting of promised calls and appointments etc.

Some firms have integrated their contact management and client management systems into a unified CRM (Client Relationship Management) system. On a firm-wide basis, managing the entire firm's selling activities enables proper sales pipeline management and forecasting systems to operate.

Information base (internal)

There is much talk about knowledge bases. However, to support professional selling there needs to be some sort of central source of information about the firm and all its services, past clients, past assignments and profiles of the various fee-earners. Manual or electronic, this information will be used to save time when professionals are preparing information packs, proposals, tender documents and presentations. Although there are set up costs, electronic information will save time and money in the long run and will result in more professional looking documents and presentations.

The key areas to address are: centralised and up-to-date CVs and/or biographies, central library of fee-earner photographs, approved client case studies, facts and figures centrally approved market sector expertise, departmental overviews, policies, recent and/or significant cases or projects.

It is also important that the firm's overall mission, financial objectives, marketing objectives, marketing strategy, competitive positioning and key messages are communicated in a concise way for all staff to understand (see Chapter two on Marketing).

External information sources

The research and preparation required for selling will be significantly easier if the firm already has access to an external information source, and even better if an information or research specialist is provided. The types of information vary enormously, from property, financial and transaction databases, searchable CD ROMs of leading business directories, on-line media reports and coverage and in-depth commercial or specially commissioned market research reports. Some services are free and need only the technology to link up, and others can be very expensive indeed. In addition, professionals will benefit from a newspaper scanning or clipping service for information on key clients, targets, markets or competitors.

Websites, multi-media and email

Increasingly, professional firms are expected to present information about their staff and services on a website. This will be particularly important for those professionals targeting overseas and technology oriented clients. An integral system will be email which also needs operational support to ensure e-mails are answered quickly. Some firms have invested heavily in multi-media design teams to allow them to produce high quality electronic documents, presentations, websites and extranets very quickly. Other firms have identified external suppliers who can provide this service.

International co-ordination

As PSFs become increasingly global there is a growing need to integrate disparate international systems – whether for contact and client management, pitch preparation or global client management plans. It is important to recognise that there are significant differences in the attitudes towards, and knowledge of, selling and marketing between American and UK firms, and also between European jurisdictions.

International and integration committees play an increasing role in international business development.

Motivation

Motivation is a huge and complex subject. There is some general information in Chapter four. A frequent request from senior and managing partners is a mechanism to improve the motivation to market and sell amongst their professional staff.

Motivation for business development can be affected by a number of organisational and individuals factors. Very often, it is not so much as improving the motivation that is required but to remove the barriers.

Typically issues affecting the motivation to develop business are:

- Too busy with client work.
- Reward system values only chargeable time (not marketing and selling).
- Risk averse culture preventing people from attempting to market and sell.
- Lack of expertise or training.
- No firm-wide guidance on the overall aims of business development.
- A lack of procedures and policies to support fee-earners who sell.

As individuals, you may need to consider the particular career aspirations – some prefer a technically oriented role, some lack essential people skills, some wish to maintain a particular work-life balance.

If you suspect that motivation is an issue, it would be wise to arrange for a representative sample of fee-earners to be interviewed on a confidential basis to identify what inhibits marketing and business development action. Then you can address the real issues.

Priorities

There is much to do in order to create an environment that is conducive to professional selling and most firms will have limited resources and therefore have to prioritise which activities will take place. It is a good idea to ensure that all the ideas and issues are debated at the outset so that an achievable plan, addressing the issues of greatest importance to your firm, is produced to guide the process.

A number of models have evolved to try to structure the various processes that must take place to support an organisation's movement from an internal product focus to an external client service focus:

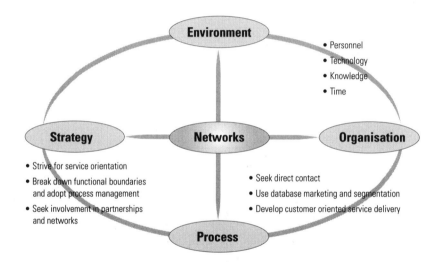

FIGURE 35: INTERNAL PROCESSES FOR THE MANAGEMENT OF EXTERNAL RELATIONSHIPS (GRONROOS)*

*Footnote: Reprinted by permission of Butterworth Heinemann Publishers, a division of Reed Educational and Professional Publishing Ltd. *CIM Handbook*

The dimensions of relationship management have been summarised as follows by Egan (CIM Handbook):

- Close client contact.
- Open systems philosophy.
- Client care mentality.
- Service culture.
- Value enhancing networks.
- Effective IT.
- Ultra customisation.
- Stakeholder orientation.
- Supply chain focus.
- Internal marketing.

My own model is as follows:

FIGURE 36: A FIRM-WIDE APPROACH TO SUPPORTING SELLING ACTIVITY

(© KIM TASSO)

Appendix 1
Sales jargon buster

Although not designed to be fully comprehensive, this 'jargon buster' or glossary, explains some of the key terms used in business development, selling and account management situations. You will need to refer to the relevant sections of the book for more explanation of the terms:

AIDA
Stands for: Attention, Interest, Desire and Action. Other variants exist – originally used to guide the development of direct mail letters.

ADVOCATE
The top stage in the CRM ladder – where a loyal client uses a variety of the service provider's services (a subscriber) and promotes the firm through referrals and recommendations.

ACCOUNT MANAGEMENT
"Account management is an approach adopted by companies aimed at building a portfolio of loyal key accounts by offering them, on a continuing basis, a service package tailored to their individual needs. To co-ordinate day-to-day interaction under the umbrella of a long-term relationship, firms typically form dedicated teams headed up by a Key Account Manager. This special treatment has significant implications for organising structure, communications and managing expectations" **(Tony Millman, 1995).**

ADVANCES
A term used in the SPIN®, model to describe where an interaction moves the buyer closer to the sale.

AUDIT (MARKETING)
A systematic approach to analysing the firm's market and marketing. See Chapter two.

B2B
Business to business – commercial client marketing.

B2C

Business to consumer – private client marketing.

BENEFIT

Something of value to a specific client in a specific situation.

BRAND

"A successful brand is an identifiable product, service, person or place augmented in such a way that the buyer or user perceives relevant, unique added values which match their needs most closely. Furthermore, its success results from being able to sustain these added values in the face of competition". **Leslie de Chernatory and Malcolm McDonald**. See Chapter two on Marketing.

CCT

Compulsory Competitive Tendering – in government clients.

CFA

Conditional Fee Arrangement.

C-LEVEL

Contact with chief operating officer or executive level – contact with board level personnel.

COACHING

"Coaching is a process that helps and supports people manage their own learning in order to maximise their potential, develop their skills, improve their performance and become the person they want to be." See Chapter nine.

COGNITIVE DISSONANCE

When an individual experiences conflict between two beliefs or between a belief and action.

COMPLEX SALE

"One in which a number of people give their approval or input before a buying decision can be made". See Chapter five.

CONTINUANCE

A term used in the SPIN®, model for when further contact is obtained but without moving closer to the sale.

CONVERSION RATE

The number of enquiries converted into business, the number of tenders won.

CPD

Continuing Professional Development.

CROSS-SELLING

A term to describe the process of encouraging an existing client to buy other services from the firm – perhaps those services provided by other departments. CRM Client Relationship Management helps – see Chapters one, two, three and eight.

DIFFERENTIATION

A key element in a marketing or sales strategy when the client is choosing on an aspect other than price. How is your offer different from your competitors? See branding and Chapter two on Marketing.

DMU

Decision-making Unit – A model to describe selling in commercial and industrial situations. The 'players' are: Gatekeepers, Users, Buyers, Influencers and Decision-makers. Later versions include sponsors (or coaches) and anti-sponsors. See Chapter five.

ELEVATOR SPEECH

Used in networking (see Chapter six) to describe the short introduction to your firm you would provide if in an elevator with a senior representative of the client for 90 seconds.

ENTRY POINT

The point at which you enter the client or prospect organisation.

EQ

Emotional intelligence. See Chapter four.

FEAST-FAMINE CYCLE

Experienced by PSF who only market when the current workload is quiet. See Chapter three.

FEATURE

Some aspect of the business or firm (that needs translating into an advantage or benefit for a particular client in a particular situation) See Chapter six on Persuasion.

GIVER'S GAIN

A networking principle. See Chapter six.

ITT

Invitation to tender – part of the competitive tendering process. See Chapter seven.

KAM

Key Account Management. See Chapter eight.

KISS

Keep It Simple Stupid – Guidance for communications and preparing presentations and tenders.

MANACT

A mnemonic to remember key questions: Money, Authority, Need, Area of interest, Competition, Timescale (©Comshare Ltd).

MARKETING

"The management process responsible for the anticipating and meeting client needs profitably" Chartered Institute of Marketing. See Chapter two.

MARKETING COMMUNICATIONS (MARCOMS)

The promotional element of the marketing mix – comprising advertising, public relations, direct marketing, sales promotion and personal selling. See Chapter two.

MARKETING MIX

The strategic mix of activities under the four (or seven) 'P' model: Product, Price, Place and Promotion (Physical evidence, Process and People). See Chapter two.

NEGOTIATION

"Conference and bargaining for mutual agreement." See Chapter six.

NICHE

A particular market segment (see segmentation). See Chapter two.

NLP

Neuro Linguistic Programming. A psychological based way of generating positive thoughts to create positive outcomes. See the books list.

NVC

Non verbal communication (body language). See Chapter six.

PERCEPTION

The process by which humans interpret information received by their senses. See Chapter four.

PERMISSION MARKETING

Where the prospect 'gives' permission to receive information from the seller, for example, by completing a registration form on a website.

PREFERENCE

Degree to which a recommender or influencer for a buyer will oppose or support your firm.

PDF

A type of computer file. It looks like a professionally designed and printed document but is viewable (but not changeable) on screen. Adobe Acrobat creates these files.

PDQF

Stands for: Plan, Demonstrate your ability, Quote and Follow up.

PEST

Political Economic Sociological Technological – Analysis tool for examining wider changes in the market and identifying future client needs. See Marketing in Chapter two.

PISTDC

A classical selling model: Prepare, Interest, Survey, Test, Demonstrate, Close (© Comshare Inc).

POST PURCHASE SATISFACTION

After making a purchase decision, the satisfaction of the buyer with that decision.

PRIMACY EFFECT

Impact of being the first argument or presentation.

PSF

Professional Service Firm.

QUALITATIVE

Where information comprises mostly subjective opinions and views – usually generated from small research studies using face-to-face interviews or focus groups. See Research in Chapter six.

QUANTITATIVE

Where information comprises mostly objective facts or numbers that can be tabulated and measured – usually generated from large-scale research studies. See Research in Chapter six.

PRIMARY RESEARCH

Sometimes called field research. This is where people are asked for their views directly. See Chapter six.

PUBLIC RELATIONS

Communicating in a structured way with all the firm's 'publics' –media (PR can mean Press Relations), staff, potential recruits, existing clients, potential clients, referrers, Government, the profession etc. See Chapter two.

RADAR™

Reading Accounts and Deploying Appropriate Resources. See Chapter six.

RELATIONSHIP MARKETING

Where selling and marketing are in the context of an ongoing relationship with a client. See Chapters one, three and eight.

RECENCY EFFECT

Impact of being the final argument or presentation.

RFP

Request for Proposal – part of the competitive tendering process. See Chapter seven.

SALES CYCLE

The period during which the sales process runs before a deal is agreed. See Chapter five.

SALES FUNNEL

Having a number of prospects and clients at each stage of the sales cycle. A concept used in Strategic Selling. See Chapter five.

SCOTSMAN

An acronym to help remember the sales process: Solution, Competitive, Originality, Timescales, Size, Money, Authority, Need.

SECONDARY RESEARCH

Sometimes called desk research, where you use information sources that have been compiled for other purposes.

SEGMENTATION

The process of breaking up a market into a number of segments that have homogeneous needs. Key segments for professional firms are private and commercial clients but these are usually divided up even further – for example, by market sector or industry, by size of client, by location of client etc. See Chapter two.

SHADOWING

Where junior or inexperienced members of staff work with senior or experienced members of staff to observe and acquire their skills.

SMART

Objectives should be: Specific Measurable Achievable Realistic and Time specific. See Chapter six.

SPIN®

Stands for: Situation, Problem, Implication and Need Payoff questions. See the books by Neil Rackman and Chapter five.

SWOT

An analysis tool – Strengths, Weaknesses, Opportunities, Threats.

TRAFFIC LIGHT ANALYSIS

A method of classifying the contacts at a client organisation (©Kim Tasso).

TOUCHPOINT

Any situation where the client comes into contact with the firm.

USP

Unique Selling Proposition.

Appendix 2
Useful sales related books

There are millions of books on the subjects of marketing, selling and client development. I have attempted to select those books that will be of most interest to the professions – rather than to marketing experts. There are further suggestions on my website at **www.kimtasso.com**.

The author accepts no liability for those books included in, or omitted from, this list. Their inclusion does not infer that they are recommended.

Specifically for the professions

CREATING NEW CLIENTS – MARKETING AND SELLING PROFESSIONAL SERVICES *Kevin Walker, Cliff Ferguson, Paul Denvir* • Cassell ISBN: 0-304-70426-1	
MANAGING KEY CLIENTS – SECURING THE FUTURE OF THE PROFESSIONAL SERVICES FIRM *Kevin Walker, Paul Denvir and Cliff Ferguson* • Continuum ISBN: 0-8264-4710-4	Latest version of *Creating new clients – marketing and selling professional services.*
TRUE PROFESSIONALISM *David H Maister* • Free Press	Although not focused on selling, the general approach to business development makes this book recommended reading. A full review is available from Kim Tasso.

MANAGING THE PROFESSIONAL SERVICE FIRM *David H Maister* • Free Press <div align="right">ISBN: 0-02-919782-1</div>	
DEVELOPING KNOWLEDGE BASED CLIENT RELATIONSHIPS – THE FUTURE OF PROFESSIONAL SERVICES *Ross Dawson* • Butterworth Heinemann <div align="right">ISBN: 0-7506-7185-8</div>	
CLIENT CARE FOR LAWYERS *Avrom Sherr* • Sweet & Maxwell <div align="right">ISBN: 0-421-57470-4</div>	
CLIENT MANAGEMENT FOR SOLICITORS *John H Freeman* • Cavendish <div align="right">ISBN: 1-85941-039-1</div>	Although not focused on selling and account management it is strongly recommended for medium sized practices. A full review is available from Kim Tasso.
SELLING SKILLS FOR PROFESSIONALS *Kim Tasso* • Thorogood <div align="right">ISBN: 1-854181-79-3</div>	The first edition of this book – in report format – that contained the results of a research exercise into attitudes towards selling in the professions.
HIGH INCOME CONSULTING – HOW TO BUILD YOUR MARKET AND YOUR PROFESSIONAL PRACTICE *Tom Lambert* • Nicholas Brealey <div align="right">ISBN: 1-85788-030-7</div>	

Marketing

MARKETING FOR LAWYERS
Matthew Moore • Gazette Practice
Handbooks   ISBN: 0-948736

One of the first books on the subject

MARKETING PROFESSIONAL SERVICES – A HANDBOOK
Patrick Forsyth • Financial Times/
Pitman Publishing   ISBN: 0-273-03849-4

MEDIA RELATIONS FOR LAWYERS
Sue Stapely • The Law Society
          ISBN: 1-85328 291 X

MARKETING IN COMMERCIAL PROPERTY
Martin Newman • Estates Gazette
          ISBN: 0 -7282-0277-8

LEGAL MARKETING
Martin Davies • Legal Practice
Handbook, Blackstone Press Ltd
          ISBN: 1-874241-3762

MARKETING COMMUNICATIONS FOR SOLICITORS
Mark Oglesby • Cavendish
Publishing Ltd   ISBN: 1-874241-19-8

PROFESSIONAL SERVICES MARKETING
Neil A Morgan • Butterworth
Heinemann   ISBN: 0-7506-0090-X

PRACTICE DEVELOPMENT – CREATING THE MARKETING MINDSET
Riskin and McKenna • Butterworths
          ISBN: 0 409 80636 6

MARKETING PROFESSIONAL SERVICES
Kotler and Bloom • Prentice Hall
ISBN: 0-13-557620-2

COMMONSENSE DIRECT MARKETING
Drayton Bird • Kogan Page
ISBN: 0-7494-3121-0

Selling frameworks

CONCEPTUAL SELLING – THE FACE-TO-FACE SALES FORMULA THAT HELPS LEADING FIRMS STAY ON TOP *Robert B Miller, Stephen Heiman* Warner Books ISBN: 0-446-38906-4	Authors of "Strategic Selling". Selected by Fortune Book Club, The Association of Sales and Marketing Book Club and The Management Book Club.
SPIN® SELLING FIELDBOOK – PRACTICAL TOOLS, METHODS, EXERCISES AND RESOURCES *Neil Rackham* • McGraw-Hill ISBN: 0-07-052235-9	SPIN® is one of the world's leading sales techniques for complex sells.
MAKING MAJOR SALES *Neil Rackman* • Gower ISBN: 0-566-02627-9	Describes the research behind the successful SPIN® technique.
THE NEW STRATEGIC SELLING – THE UNIQUE SALES SYSTEM PROVEN SUCCESSFUL BY THE WORLD'S BEST FIRMS *Stephen E Heiman, Diane Sanchez* Warner Books ISBN: 0-446-67346-3	Strategic Selling is a leading sales framework. This book is recommended.
HOPE IS NOT A STRATEGY – SIX WAYS TO WINNING THE COMPLEX SALE *Rick Page* • Nautilus Press ISBN: 0-9669102-4-9	

For experienced sales people

SELLING WITH INTEGRITY – **REINVENTING SALES THROUGH** **COLLABORATION, RESPECT AND** **SERVING** *Sharon Drew* • Morgen Berrett Koehler <div align="right">ISBN: 1-57675-017-5</div>	New York Times Business Best-seller.
EMPATHY SELLING – THE POWERFUL **NEW SALES TECHNIQUE FOR THE 1990s** *Christopher C Golis* Kogan Page ISBN: 0-7494-0969-X	A personal favourite of the author.

Selling skills

INTERPERSONAL COMMUNICATION *Peter Hartley* • Routledge <div align="right">ISBN: 0-415-01385-2</div>	
THE HANDBOOK OF **COMMUNICATION SKILLS** *Bernice Hurst* • Kogan Page	
EFFECTIVE SPEAKING *Cristina Stuart* • Pan ISBN: 0-330-29868-2	An excellent UK book. Their organisation provides training as well.
EFFECTIVE LISTENING SKILLS *Dennis M Kratz, Abbey Robinson Kratz* Irwin ISBN: 0-7863-0122-8	
MAKING SUCCESSFUL PRESENTATIONS *Patrick Forsyth* • Sheldon <div align="right">ISBN: 0-85969-725-8</div>	Kim Tasso has a full review on this book.

CONFIDENT CONVERSATION: HOW TO TALK IN ANY BUSINESS OR SOCIAL SITUATION

Dr Lillian Glass • Judy Piatkus

ISBN: 0-7499-1081-X

CONFIDENT PUBLIC SPEAKING – HOW TO COMMUNICATE EFFECTIVELY USING THE POWERTALK SYSTEM

Christian H Godefroy, Stephanie Barrat

Piatkus ISBN: 0-7499-1827-6

PUTTING IT ACROSS – THE ART OF COMMUNICATING, PERSUADING AND PRESENTING

Angela Heylin • Michael Joseph

ISBN: 0-7181-3451-6

Account management

RELATIONSHIP MARKETING

Regis McKenna • Century Business

ISBN: 0-7126-5563-8

SUCCESSFUL LARGE ACCOUNT MANAGEMENT

Robert B Miller, Stephen E Heiman

Warner Books ISBN: 0-446-39356-8

RELATIONSHIP MARKETING – BRINGING QUALITY, CUSTOMER SERVICE AND MARKETING TOGETHER

Martin Christopher, Adrian Payne and David Ballantyne • Butterworth Heinemann ISBN: 0-7506-0978-8

KEY ACCOUNT MANAGEMENT – LEARNING FROM SUPPLIER AND CUSTOMER PERSPECTIVES *Malcolm McDonald, Beth Rogers* Butterworth Heinemann ISBN: 0-7506-3278-X	
KEY ACCOUNT MANAGERS POCKETBOOK *Roger E Jones* • Management Pocketbooks　ISBN: 1-870471-42-3	
COMPETITIVE TENDERING **Win that pitch! How to secure new business and keep clients** *Quentin Bell* • Kogan Page ISBN: 0-7494-0692-5	Author is a leading PR practitioner.
PROPOSALS PITCHES AND BEAUTY PARADES *John de Forte, Guy Jones* • Financial Times Pitman　ISBN: 0-273-60170-9	UK authors are experienced in the professions (especially accountants). A full review is available from Kim Tasso. Recommended reading.

Negotiation

NEGOTIATE – THE ART OF WINNING *Harry A Mills* • BCA　ISBN: 9 780566 072871	
GETTING TO YES – NEGOTIATING AN AGREEMENT WITHOUT GIVING IN *Roger Fisher and William Ury* Arrow　ISBN: 0-09-924842-5	

Non verbal communication/Psychology

BODY LANGUAGE – HOW TO MAKE THE MOST OF YOUR PERSONAL ASSETS BY READING AND USING THE BODY'S SECRET SIGNALS

Susan Quilliam • Carlton

ISBN: 1-85868-075-1

BODYTALK – A WORLD GUIDE TO GESTURES

Desmond Morris

Random House   ISBN: 0-224-03969-5

BODY LANGUAGE – HOW TO READ OTHERS' THOUGHTS BY THEIR GESTURES

Allan Pease • Sheldon   ISBN: 0-85969-782-7

SECRET LANGUAGE OF SUCCESS – HOW TO READ AND USE BODY TALK

Dr David Lewis • Guild Publishing

ISBN: 0-593-01491-X

NLP – THE NEW ART AND SCIENCE OF GETTING WHAT YOU WANT

Dr Harry Alder

Piatkus   ISBN: 0-7499-1430-0

NLP is not a sales framework but assists with developing confidence.

DEVELOP YOUR NLP SKILLS

Andrew Bradbury • Kogan Page/

Sunday Times   ISBN: 0-7494-3260-8

NLP – THE NEW TECHNOLOGY OF ACHIEVEMENT

Steve Andreas and Charles Faulkner

Nicholas Brealey   ISBN: 1-85788-122-2

NLP is not a sales framework but assists with developing confidence.

Miscellaneous

SELLING SERVICES AND PRODUCTS – A PICTORIAL GUIDE *Malcolm H B McDonald and Peter Morris* Butterworth Heinemann <div align="right">ISBN: 0-7506-0069-1</div>	McDonald is a leading marketing expert.
THE CIM HANDBOOK OF SELLING AND SALES STRATEGY *David Jobber* • Butterworth Heinemann <div align="right">ISBN: 0-7506-3116-3</div>	
HOW TO SELL A SERVICE – GUIDELINES FOR EFFECTIVE SELLING IN A SERVICE BUSINESS *Malcolm H B McDonald, John Leppard* Heinemann ISBN: 0-434-91288-3	McDonald is a leading marketing expert.
TEACH YOURSELF SELLING *Jean Atkinson* Hodder & Stoughton ISBN: 0-340-72053-0	Basic introduction particularly useful for those selling recruitment services.
ALL ABOUT SELLING *Alan Williams* McGraw-Hill ISBN: 0-07-08493-X	This is an old book and more oriented to the classical (as opposed to the consultative) style of selling.
HOW TO WIN FRIENDS AND INFLUENCE PEOPLE *Dale Carnegie* Worlds Work ISBN: 437-02072-X	Yes, it is ancient but it still holds valuable lessons for interpersonal communication.
KISS, BOW OR SHAKE HANDS *Terri Monson, Wayne A Conaway and George A Borden* • Bob Adams Inc <div align="right">ISBN: 1-55850-444-3</div>	A great book if you regularly meet people to do business from overseas.

SEVEN HABITS OF HIGHLY EFFECTIVE PEOPLE	A great general book for improving your day-to-day effectiveness (and creating more time for selling!)
Stephen Covey	
SUNDAY TIMES – HOW TO MANAGE ORGANIZATIONAL CHANGE	
D E Hussey	
Kogan Page ISBN: 0-7494-3251-9	

What's your favourite selling book? Do you have a view on any of the books mentioned?

Do you have a better suggestion? Are there any other reference documents you found particularly useful? Who provides the best sales training for the professions? Better still, what on-line resources have you come to use?

Please let me have your ideas and I will post them on a website (email: kim@kimtasso.com) – and attribute your comments, if you wish.

Appendix 3
Self-appraisal of service performance

For further information on when and how to use a client management team you might use this self assessment questionnaire as part of the account management process. Please refer to Chapter eight – Account management.

To be completed by each member of the major client or account team in advance of the first team meeting.

Client _____

Your name_____ Date_____

Q1 Rank the key attributes in the table below in the order of the importance for this client, where 1 is most valued and 16 is least valued by this client.

Q2 Evaluate your perceptions of the team's performance on each of the key attributes by placing a tick in the most appropriate column. Note any points or comments you want to share with the team.

see opposite...

	Q1	Q2				
	RANK (or select the most important for your client)	VERY GOOD	GOOD	OK	POOR	VERY POOR
1. Partners are easily accessible						
2. Partners thoroughly understand the client's business – day-to-day pressures, long-term issues, their organisation and their industry						
3. Partners offer commercial advice and do not limit their advice to strictly legal/ accountant/property/ technical issues						
4. Partners are proactive – e.g. they call the client up to talk about industry issues and clip relevant items from the press						
5. The assistants thoroughly understand the client's business						
6. The team offers insights to the client						
7. The client gets the same level of service no matter who on the team is working for them						

	Q1	Q2				
	RANK (or select the most important for your client)	VERY GOOD	GOOD	OK	POOR	VERY POOR
8. Our team provides real expertise in the areas where the client needs it						
9. Our team produces documents and materials that exactly match the client's requirements						
10. Our team achieves standards that are consistently high						
11. The client enjoys working with us and feels they have a good, open and productive relationship						
12. The client gets a fast response						
13. All the client's work is co-ordinated and supervised through a central point						
14. The client knows a number of people at the firm and knows who to call on different issues						
15. The client receives value for money						

	Q1	Q2				
	RANK (or select the most important for your client)	**VERY GOOD**	**GOOD**	**OK**	**POOR**	**VERY POOR**
16. We are innovative in serving this client						
17. We are making the best use of technology in supporting this client						
18. The client's attitude to the way we charge for and bill for work is positive						
19. The client perceives that all the services and facilities (e.g. technology, knowledge, secretarial support, training etc.) of the firm are available to them in a way that is beneficial						
20. The client has a good understanding of the other aspects, services, expertise and facilities available across the firm						
21. The client believes that we have done our best to identify and provide joint and other opportunities, to help them pursue their business goals						

Q3 In view of the perceived importance of each attribute for this client and your perception of the team's performance, provide a very brief explanation of any particular strengths or weaknesses which this exercise has highlighted.

Q4 Please provide a brief narrative appraisal of the client service team's overall performance.

Q5 Please list any actions which should be implemented to enhance your client service approach.

Account partner only:

Q6 What are the key findings and actions that emerge from the team's discussion of the self-appraisal?

Q7 To what extent does the team's combined assessment of the level of service and satisfaction of this client relate to what you have learned from the client at the external or internal service review? If a client service review has not yet taken place, when is it scheduled to take place and what specific issues will you be raising with the client?

Appendix 4
Internal service review questionnaire and example questions

Further information about how and when to use this questionnaire is available in Chapter eight on Account management.

The following proforma may be helpful to guide the discussion at an internal service review. Please read Chapter eight to help you prepare for the meeting and to complete the necessary actions after the meeting. However, if the client wishes to discuss any other issues, or to focus on any specific issues, then these should take precedence over the checklist below.

Although it is not always possible, by asking the client to rate their level of satisfaction (e.g. 1 = highly dissatisfied and 5 = highly satisfied), you may be able to better identify those areas requiring more in-depth discussion.

DISCUSSION TOPICS	RATING	CLIENT COMMENTS	ACTIONS, RESPONSIBILITIES, TIMING
Current business situation Start the conversation by asking the client to talk about the general issues affecting: a) Their industry b) Their organisation c) Their department/team Ask them to describe the three biggest challenges that they face			
Working relationship The following areas should be explored: • Anticipating their needs • Accessibility and ease of contact • Commercial awareness • Understanding of their business • Friendliness of partners and staff • Amount of social contact • Speed of response • Regularity of contact • Meeting deadlines • Ideas and innovation • Proactivity • Use of technology • Progress review and audit meetings			

DISCUSSION TOPICS	RATING	CLIENT COMMENTS	ACTIONS, RESPONSIBILITIES, TIMING

Communicating with the firm
Mention some of the following areas to prompt discussion about communications
 	
• Answering telephone calls
 	
• Taking and returning messages
 	
• Electronic communication
 	
• Correspondence
 	
• Books
 	
• Market research/general information
 	
• Keeping you informed
   – Day-to-day discussions
 	
• Updates on fee position
 	
• Updates on market developments
 	
• Seminars and briefings
   – Training courses
 	
• The website
   – Extranets
 	
   – Client partner/account partner communication
 	
   – Expressions of dissatisfaction or complaints
 	
   – The firm's marketing programmes
 	
   – With other departments and offices of the firm (explore international associations and offices if relevant)			

DISCUSSION TOPICS	RATING	CLIENT COMMENTS	ACTIONS, RESPONSIBILITIES, TIMING
Ask the client what additional information, marketing or contacts would be useful to them			
Satisfaction with current members of the team Ask the client to comment on the performance of individual members of the team • Account partner • Account manager • Key contact 1 • Key contact 2 • Others			
Quality of service provided by different specialist teams You should know in advance which areas the client is likely to have comments on: • List of specialist services or departments			
Propensity to use services not currently used Mention any services or areas of expertise that the client is not currently using to assess the likelihood of them using them in the future: • List of specialist services or departments			

DISCUSSION TOPICS	RATING	CLIENT COMMENTS	ACTIONS, RESPONSIBILITIES, TIMING
Quality of service provided by the various offices: • List of domestic offices • List of overseas offices			
Overall satisfaction As a summary of the discussion return to the broader issues of the service provided: • Expertise • Quality of advice • Commercial awareness • Relationship • Market knowledge • Reputation • Performance • Compared to similar firms • Value for money			
At the end of the discussion, you should check whether there are any other ways in which we could improve the service provided			
Ask how else the relationship could be strengthened and improved			

Checklist of open-ended question probes

In addition to the questionnaire above, you may find the following questions helpful in getting clients to open up and discuss issues in more detail. Another useful technique is to ask for examples of particularly good or poor performance:

Performance and improvement

- What are the main criteria on which you judge performance?
- What are your expectations of us?
- Against these criteria, how do we perform?
- What are the gaps?
- What are our strengths and weaknesses?
- How constructive and commercial is our advice?
- How do we compare with other advisers?
- Do we provide innovative solutions rather than problems?
- Have you experienced any problems in the past 12 months?
- How did you rate our performance on the last transaction/deal/audit etc?
- Have we resolved them to your satisfaction? What else should we do?

Different departments and offices

- To what extent is the level of service consistent across departments and offices?
- How well do you feel our departments and offices work together?

Team and working relationship

- How would you describe the working relationship between our teams?
- In what ways does the working relationship need to be changed or improved?
- How can we keep you better informed of progress?
- How can we adapt the information and services we provide better to suit your systems and processes?
- How can we make the teams work more closely and effectively?
- How well does the team understand your business and industry?
- How can we improve our understanding?
- Who are the strongest (and weakest) members of the team?
- How can we improve the team?
- What gaps exist in our skill, experience or expertise?
- How consistent is the level of service provided across team members?
- What are your views on our succession planning?

Responsive and proactive

- How easy is it to gain access to team members?
- How good (or bad) are we at meeting deadlines?
- Are we generally fast or slow to respond?
- How proactive are we?
- In which areas would you appreciate greater responsiveness?
- In which areas would you appreciate greater innovation?
- What new services might you be interested in?
- What solutions have we provided to your organisation?

Added value

- Which aspects of our service or our relationship with you provide the greatest value to your organisation?
- To what extent do we add value?
- What additional help, or benefits, or service would you appreciate?
- To what extent do team members 'go the extra mile'?

Entertaining, publications and seminars

- How are our publications and events perceived?
- What methods of entertaining do you most value?
- To what extent do you use our website and/or extranets and how can these be improved for you?
- How do they compare with what you receive from other advisers?
- How could they be improved?
- What is of most value to your organisation?
- What additional publications or events should we provide?
- What type of event is most appreciated by your organisation?
- What are the best dates and times to organise events?
- To what extent does your organisation prefer formal to informal events?

Fees

- To what extent do you feel you receive added value from us?
- How do we compare on fees with other advisers?
- Are there other methods of pricing, billing or cost control that you would like us to explore?
- Do we provide all the necessary information?
- Which areas of fees cause concern?
- How could we improve your satisfaction with the fees?

Future relationship

- How integral is our service to your overall business success?
- To what extent are we the first port of call for advice?
- How can we increase the strength and value of our relationship?
- Are there any areas where you would not seek advice from us?
- In what ways could we collaborate on mutual opportunities?
- How well positioned are we with all the key individuals at your organisation?
- To what extent do we maintain the right level of formal and informal communication with your organisation?
- What can we do to extend and improve the relationship between our organisations?
- What changes in your industry or business do you foresee that will impact on our relationship?
- What additional services or expertise should we provide for you?
- How can we use technology to strengthen and expand the services we provide to you?

Appendix 5
Full account management plan

**Chapter eight is concerned with the account management process –
and it is recommended that all the work you do for a particular major
client or account as part of the process is summarised in a plan. You
should read Chapter eight before attempting to use this outline account
management plan.**

After the team exercise on self-appraisal, the external or internal service
review and any other research on the client's organisation or industry, this
outline plan should be completed by the account manager with assistance
from the account partner – it provides a structured approach to assessing
the client's needs and team's position at present, setting key objectives and
planning both service and business development actions for the future.

The more time that is spent collecting information and assessing the present
position, the better the resulting plan and subsequent account management
success. Completing the plan should enable every member of the account
team to develop a deep and thorough knowledge of the firm's past
relationship with the client, the specific needs and issues relating to the
servicing of the client and the planned future approach.

Where questions are not relevant to your particular client, feel free to leave
them out. If there are other issues that are relevant to your client which are
not covered by the questions, there is a space towards the end for these to
be noted. You may need the assistance of the marketing, finance, human
resources and IT teams to complete some parts of the plan.

Where you are dealing with particularly large, complex or international
clients it may be necessary to produce a plan for individuals regions or
divisions of the client. However, it is important that someone within the
firm is aware of the separate plans and is able to provide an integrating
and co-ordinating role.

The plan is a living document designed to help you manage the client on a day-to-day basis – it is therefore important that the team understands all the issues and feels that the plan is for their use, rather than for anyone else at the firm. The document will also prove valuable to any new members of the firm or team, who are required to work on the client's behalf. Set a date by which the plan will be completed.

---

1 Client overview

Client organisation name _____

Plan for year ending _____

Client turnover _____

Client number of staff _____

Client business sector _____

Nature of business _____

Year established _____

Holding company/subsidiaries _____

Legal status _____

Other comments _____

_____

Accountants _____

Lawyers _____

Bankers _____

Property advisers _____

Date became client _____

Last year's fee income _____

Last year's profitability _____

---

2 Team overview

Account partner _____

Account manager _____

Team members _____

_____

_____

(Be sure to indicate the different departments and locations of the team members.)

2.1. Is the present team structure appropriate? If not, what changes or enhancements are required?

2.2. Is there consistency of client contact? How well does the client know each of the team members?

2.3. Are there other members of the firm that should be introduced to the client?

2.4. Other comments about the team?

3 Client operations

The overall aim of this section is to aid the identification of opportunities to enhance client service as well as opportunities to cross-sell and any risks to the firm. By fully understanding the operations of the client you can identify opportunities to assist in the future development of the business – both from observations made by the team and by the introduction of relevant specialists, or the use of external information sources or contacts. You may find help in the selling frameworks section of the book in Chapter five.

3.1. Note down any key developments in the client's industry that may have an impact on their future operations.

3.2. Are there any relevant competitive issues that the client faces?

3.3. Does the client's financial reports and accounts reveal anything that is important for the team to be aware of?

3.4. Identify any major strengths, weaknesses, opportunities or threats that the client faces.

3.5. Note down any significant changes that the client has undertaken (e.g. mergers, acquisitions, restructuring etc.) over the past three years.

3.6. Note down any significant changes that the client is likely to undertake over the next three years.

3.7. Identify any areas or issues that the firm should explore further to better understand the client's business and suggest ways this information could be obtained (e.g. subscribe to trade journals, press coverage, annual report, on-line information services, membership of industry associations, other contacts at the firm etc.).

4 Relationships

Prepare and attach an organisation chart that maps out:

a) where the firm has existing contact or relationships at the client organisation

b) where the firm knows there are individuals with which it should form relationships

c) where the firm lacks knowledge of the relevant individuals in a particular part of the client's organisation.

4.1. What actions need to be taken to strengthen or develop relationships with the client?

4.2. In what ways do the various contacts at the client have different expectations and experiences of the firm?

4.3. Do any of these people have relationships with other competitor firms? If so, describe briefly.

5 Service

5.1. Why and how did the client originally come to use the firm? Note the names of any referrers, or particular reasons, the names of former advisers etc.

5.2. From the service self-appraisal team exercise, note down any key issues or topics that should be tackled over the next 12 months.

5.3. Describe the services of the firm that the client has used in the past.

5.4. Describe the services of the firm that are being used by the client at present.

5.5. Are there any international issues relating to this client? If so, note down how this is serviced at present and any changes that need to be made.

5.6. Does the client use other advisers for any part of their work? If so note down who they use, and for what, and estimate the likely annual fees that go to these other advisers. Indicate the likelihood or desirability, of the firm getting this work.

5.7. To what extent are other value added, but perhaps non-chargeable, services provided to this client (e.g. training, seminars, secondments etc.).

5.8. What opportunities are there for increasing the efficiency of the service provided or extending the value of the service provided (e.g. through the use of technology) for this client?

5.9. What new services or delivery methods should be produced for this client?

6 Fees and budgets

Indicate the fee income and profitability of this client's work over the past three years and the targets for this year.

It is advisable to provide a detailed table of the fees and profits from this client – by service area and office if relevant – to obtain an overview of all activity between the client and the firm.

7 Objectives

Bearing in mind the preceding analysis, the feedback from the client service reviews and the financial targets set for this client, list the three main objectives for account management and development this year and for the longer term. Objectives should be specific, measurable and time specific and you may want to consider strategic objectives for the firm as well as those to do with relationship, cross-selling and competitive issues at the client.

This year:

1. _____

2. _____

3. _____

Longer term:

1. _____

2. _____

3. _____

8 Action plan

This is the most important part of the account management plan as it will drive the action for all members of the team over the next 12 months. It will be used to monitor progress against the objectives and targets that have been set and will allocate the various tasks amongst all team members. Typical sections of an action plan might be:

8.1. Research/background knowledge issues.

8.2. Team issues.

8.3. Relationship and networking issues.

8.4. Service issues.

8.5. Fees, budgets, credit control and billing issues.

8.6. Entertaining, business development and marketing issues.

8.7. Other account management or development issues.

9 Any other comments or issues of relevance to this client?

_____

_____

_____

_____

_____

_____

_____

_____

Appendix 6
Summary account management plan

You should refer to Chapter eight on Account management before using this outline plan. If you have been through the full account management process, or if for some reason, you have insufficient time or resources to complete a full account management plan (see Appendix five) then the following summary plan outline might be used. This is the bare minimum required for each major client of the firm.

Client name: _____

Account partner: _____

Account manager:_____

Date completed: _____

OBJECTIVES	STRATEGIES	TACTICS			
		Q1	Q2	Q3	Q4
1.	A.				
	B.				
	C.				
2.	A.				
	B.				
	C.				
3.	A.				
	B.				
	C.				
4.	A.				
	B.				
	C.				
5.	A.				
	B.				
	C.				
6.	A.				
	B.				
	C.				
7.	A.				
	B.				
	C.				
OTHER KEY DATES					

Appendix 7
Checklist: Are you ready to sell?

STAGE	TASK	RELEVANT CHAPTERS IN THIS BOOK	TICK WHEN COMPLETED
Your attitude	Feel positive about selling?	1. Introduction. 3. What is selling?	
	Feel and look confident about selling?	Chapters one and three for general information about selling in the professions. 6. Selling skills (Non verbal communication).	
	Motivated to sell?	Motivation is covered in Chapters four and nine.	
Your training	Learn more about selling?	All sections.	
	Identified specific weaknesses to address with focused training?	6. Selling skills. 9. Firm-wide issues on selling (training).	
	Selected an appropriate selling framework and sought training in that framework?	5. Selling frameworks. 9. Firm-wide issues on selling (training).	
	Studied the aspects of selling that are of most interest to you?	See the book list in Appendix 2.	
	Got some practice		

STAGE	TASK	RELEVANT CHAPTERS IN THIS BOOK	TICK WHEN COMPLETED
Your firm	Checked your firm's expectations, attitudes to and resources for selling?	9. Firm-wide issues on selling.	
Your knowledge	Learned about your firm's services?		
	Learn about your competitors?		
	Learned about your firm's track record with the types of clients you are targeting?		
Your marketing plan	Developed a marketing plan?	1. Introduction 2. Marketing	
Your sales plan	Set some objectives	6. Selling skills (Objectives)	
	Develop a target list within the context of a plan	6. Selling skills (targeting)	
	Research your targets	6. Selling skills (researching)	
	Create a system to support your sales and contact management and account management efforts	9. Firm-wide issues on selling (Systems)	
	Develop empathy with your clients and targets	4. Adopting the buyer's point of view	
	Identify your key existing clients and prepare account management plans	8. Account management Appendices	

Get selling!

Thorogood publishing

Thorogood publishes a wide range of books, reports, special briefings, psychometric tests and videos. Listed below is a selection of key titles.

Desktop Guides

The marketing strategy desktop guide — *Norton Paley* • £16.99

The sales manager's desktop guide — *Mike Gale and Julian Clay* • £16.99

The company director's desktop guide — *David Martin* • £16.99

The credit controller's desktop guide — *Roger Mason* • £16.99

The company secretary's desktop guide — *Roger Mason* • £16.99

The finance and accountancy desktop guide — *Ralph Tiffin* • £16.99

The commercial engineer's desktop guide — *Tim Boyce* • £16.99

The training manager's desktop guide — *Eddie Davies* • £16.99

The PR practitioner's desktop guide — *Caroline Black* • £16.99

Win new business – the desktop guide — *Susan Croft* • £16.99

Masters in Management

Mastering business planning and strategy — *Paul Elkin* • £19.99

Mastering financial management — *Stephen Brookson* • £19.99

Mastering leadership — *Michael Williams* • £19.99

Mastering marketing — *Ian Ruskin-Brown* • £22.00

Mastering negotiations — *Eric Evans* • £19.99

Mastering people management	*Mark Thomas* • £19.99
Mastering personal and interpersonal skills	*Peter Haddon* • £16.99
Mastering project management	*Cathy Lake* • £19.99

Business Action Pocketbooks

Edited by David Irwin

Building your business pocketbook	£10.99
Developing yourself and your staff pocketbook	£10.99
Finance and profitability pocketbook	£10.99
Managing and employing people pocketbook	£10.99
Sales and marketing pocketbook	£10.99
Managing projects and operations pocketbook	£9.99
Effective business communications pocketbook	£9.99
PR techniques that work	*Edited by Jim Dunn* • £9.99
Adair on leadership	*Edited by Neil Thomas* • £9.99

Other titles

The John Adair handbook of management and leadership	*Edited by Neil Thomas* • £29.95
The inside track to successful management	*Dr Gerald Kushel* • £16.95
The pension trustee's handbook (3rd edition)	*Robin Ellison* • £25
Boost your company's profits	*Barrie Pearson* • £12.99
Negotiate to succeed	*Julie Lewthwaite* • £12.99

The management tool kit   *Sultan Kermally* • £10.99

Working smarter   *Graham Roberts-Phelps* • £15.99

Test your management skills   *Michael Williams* • £12.99

The art of headless chicken management
Elly Brewer and Mark Edwards • £6.99

EMU challenge and change – the implications for business
John Atkin • £11.99

Everything you need for an NVQ in management
Julie Lewthwaite • £19.99

Customer relationship management   *Graham Roberts-Phelps* • £12.99

Time management and personal development
John Adair and Melanie Allen • £9.99

Sales management and organisation   *Peter Green* • £9.99

Telephone tactics   *Graham Roberts-Phelps* • £9.99

Companies don't succeed people do!   *Graham Roberts-Phelps* • £12.99

Inspiring leadership   *John Adair* • £24.99

The book of ME   *Barrie Pearson and Neil Thomas* • £24.99

The complete guide to debt recovery   *Roger Mason* • £12.99

Janner's speechmaker   *Greville Janner* • £12.99

Gurus on business strategy   *Tony Grundy* • £14.99

Thorogood also has an extensive range of reports and special briefings which are written specifically for professionals wanting expert information.

For a full listing of all Thorogood publications, or to order any title, please call Thorogood Customer Services on 020 7749 4748 or fax on 020 7729 6110. Alternatively view our website at **www.thorogood.ws**.